Praise for *Holding My Hand Through Hell*

"*Holding My Hand Through Hell* is a harrowing true story of violence and survival. The specter of Susan Murphy Milano's abusive father followed her into adulthood, and the mental anguish she experienced would have destroyed most of us, but she persevered. This is an inspirational story that should be read by everyone."

—Anthony Bruno, author, *The Iceman: The True Story of a Cold-Blooded Killer* and *Seven*

"Susan Milano Murphy is a warrior for those whose lives have been touched by violent crime. She writes from the heart -- because she's been there herself. A must read!"

—Gregg Olsen, *New York Times* best selling author, including *Starvation Heights*

"A gripping and tragic true tale of abuse, murder, healing, and faith. Susan Murphy Milano puts her heart and soul into this book and it shows. Highly recommended."

—R. Barri Flowers, author, *The Sex Slave Murders* and over 40 other books

"You will be compelled to look closer into the horror of intimate partner abuse and the shear madness of our incompetence to protect those who are harassed, threatened, beaten, and those who ultimately wind up on a Missing Person flyer."

—Kim Anklin, Senior Investigative Analyst of Management Resources LTD of NY

"I felt, from the very first page, that I was sitting having coffee with her in a kitchen as she retold her story. She writes with a rawness and eloquence that is the hallmark of an excellent scribe and with the love and tenderness of a child. A daughter who would stop at nothing to exorcise her demons and make advocacy for crime victims her life's very important work. We need more Susan's in the world. She brought me to my knees, brought me to tears, and made me want to be a better person as I read about her journey. She is a hero to many, but an ordinary person who became an extraordinary voice. Everyone who cares about human beings and faith and family should pick up this crucial book. Bravo, Susan! Your legacy will be that of love, caring, and the journey to forgiveness despite the darkest days anyone could live"

—Liz Seccuro, victims' rights activist and author, *Crash Into Me: A Survivor's Search for Justice*

"Riveting and heart wrenching, Susan takes us on a captivating, gritty journey from vulnerability and victimhood to victory over abuse by sharing some of the most intimate details of her own unthinkable tragedies. Her work gives us a front row seat into her personal tale of terror, and provides first hand insight into a terribly broken system of protection from domestic abuse and violence at its worst. More importantly, Susan furnishes the blueprints for escape to others who are similarly trapped when the system is absent or otherwise silent. A brilliant tale from the front lines. You won't be able to put it down."

—Douglas J. Hagmann, investigator, author, & talk show host

"Susan Murphy Milano's childhood journey is not one filled with joyful noises and playful things. Survival mode was a way of life. The abuse and losses continued to mount in adulthood. Despite everything, she has risen above the depths of hell on earth to continue her mission to help others and herself in the process. This book shines a floodlight on domestic violence and is an outstanding public service to all, a true work of art!"

  —Donna R. Gore, MA, Crime Survivor and Victims'
  Rights Advocate

"Susan's heart beautifully shines through in her story. *Holding My Hand Through Hell* is honest and heartfelt, and if you allow it to, it will change your life. *Holding My Hand Through Hell* is Susan's compelling look at all of the distinct and painful angles of domestic violence. In the end, you will be left with a tremendous sense of hope. While mincing no words, Susan gives a beautiful voice to the supremely ugly epidemic of family violence. This book is a must-read for victims and also for their advocates. I pray that Susan's story would give many other women back the voices that were stolen from them because of domestic violence. Susan's pain has become her passion and calling. I'm blessed to work with Susan and to be her fellow justice-seeker. Truly, the Lord has held Susan's hand through hell, and her story will offer that same hand of hope to many others"

  —Neil Schori, Lead Pastor/Advocate, Napierville
  Christian Church

"Susan Murphy Milano's book paints a vivid up close picture of domestic violence. You feel this book on a gut level and you understand like never before the culture of indifference and secrecy surrounding domestic violence. Her story is an example of how perpetrators are protected and victims are victimized by the very system designed to help them. Yet Murphy Milano rises above her harrowing upbringing, and turns tragedy into triumph as she becomes a pioneer in the crusade for justice, shining a light on the dark, secretive world of batterers and their victims. Even though Murphy Milano escapes the abuse of her childhood, she continues to attract it in her adult relationships. Ultimately, she learns to spot that the pattern ingrained in childhood lives within. Once she frees herself from her dangerous relationships, she understands she is ultimately responsible for her own life with God's help. This book is a must read on domestic violence."

—Susan F. Filan, Esq., is a former CT state prosecutor, MSNBC-TV Senior Legal Analyst, and an experienced trial lawyer

"A compelling story of her own victimization at the hands of a very pathological parent. However, the redeeming aspects of this story are highlighted by the determination of a survivor to positively impact the field of victimology through a lifetime of service. The field, and the world, is blessed to have a thriver like Susan hold other victim's hand through their own personal hell. This is a powerful story demonstrating how others can use their own pain for other's gain."

—Sandra L. Brown, MA, & CEO, The Institute for Relational Harm Reduction & Public Pathology Education; Board of Directors for End Violence Against Women International

"Susan expertly crafts her story in a way that transforms one woman's human tragedies into a soulful inspirational story of perpetual hope, grace, and godly salvation. Her words will encourage all of us to seek a higher power bigger than our devastating tribulations we all face along this journey together."

—Jillian Maas Backman, author, *Beyond the Pews: Breaking With Tradition and Letting Go of Religious Lockdown*

"Susan Murphy Milano has skillfully allowed readers the privilege of learning the genesis of tireless labors on behalf of victims of domestic violence in her latest work, *Holding My Hand Through Hell* as readers learn exactly what it was that shaped her adult life and gave her the passion to see those in harm's way brought to harbor. Well written and fast paced, Murphy Milano has given to all concerned with the violence that destroys lives, an inside, honest, painful, but necessary understanding of the dynamics in the home, as well as the burdens carried by those who remain in the wake of destruction. By allowing us to know what factors made Milano into who she is today, a tireless advocate for victims, she allows us to see more about ourselves, and why we care for those who remain at risk. Essential reading."

—Peter Hyatt, Statement Analyist

"Susan literally stands in front of you with her emotional pants down and walks you through all the smells, heartaches, anger, fears of her life then shares how she pieced her crushed life back together again. Susan Murphy Milano has done it, given us all a vivid and gutsy book that forges a bold path toward healing, safety, and hope. Bravo Susan!"

—Dr. Laurie Roth, PhD and host, The Laurie Roth Show

"A riveting book. The raw prose describes in frightening detail the effect that living in a torture chamber has on fragile children. With courageous honesty Susan Murphy-Milano bears her soul and exposes family secrets at great personal cost. Murphy-Milano is proof that despite the trauma her law enforcement abuser inflicted on her, there is survival, there is achievement, there is a life of making a difference possible, and most importantly, there is hope. This story is a testament to the strength of the human spirit and what one can accomplish when they refuse to let their abuser have power over them. A worthwhile read for anyone!"

—Holly B. Hughes, Attorney at Law, CNN & HLN
Legal Analyst, and Tru TV contributor.

"Susan Murphy-Milano's childhood was terrorized by her police detective father—a monster who violated women and children, including those in the neighborhood. When he ultimately took the life of Susan's mother she was left with the bloody wreckage to salvage. But Susan didn't crumble. She gleaned strength and courage from her experience and transformed her violent past into a lifelong passion to help other women suffering from abuse. Blessings to you, Susan, for working so hard for so many for so long."

—Dawn Schiller, author, *The Road Through Wonderland: Surviving John Holmes* and founder of E.S.T.E.A.M.

"I highly recommend *Holding My Hand Through Hell*, not only to all survivors, but also to all working toward creating a safer, more peaceful world. This is beautifully written book that describes suffering, but ends in hope.

—Dr. Renee Fredickson, Psychologist

"The most common question we hear about domestic violence is why does *she* stay. In her new book, Susan Murphy-Milano illustrates the answer to this question, but she does much more. She demonstrates why this is the wrong question because it focuses on approaches that blame the victim. A better and more interesting question would be why would an abuser repeatedly hurt the woman he claims to love more than any other? Ultimately Susan brings us to the best question—Why does society continue to permit men to abuse their partners and their children? This book will help women partnered with abusers and protective mothers to use the safest practices available when they try to escape. They will be inspired as I was by the examples Susan provides, but most of all Susan Murphy-Milano brings us closer to ending domestic violence by focusing on why society continues to allow abusive men to ruin the lives of so many people."

—Barry Goldstein, Esq., author, *Scared To Leave, Afraid To Stay: Paths From Family Violence To Safety*

"A first hand, true story which only Susan Murphy Milano could tell! Her style allows the reader to witness the drama and the abuse, up close, as if you were there in the same setting while the acts unfold. Many a reader will empathize with the characters in the story, however, a much larger number of readers will recognize the same controlling behavior, so clearly detailed, and realize that Susan is describing events that are occurring in their own lives or that of close friends. It is to those people that the lesson can be learned—there is a way out of Hell!"

—Dr. Michael Berkland, D.O., Forensic Pathologist, Crime Scene Analyst

"Susan Murphy Milano's latest offering is a gripping story of domestic violence that could only be told by someone who witnessed intimate partner abuse first hand. Based on Susan's real life experiences, this book takes the reader on a journey through the dark side of human behavior and back into the light. After reading this book it will be clear why Susan became the tireless victims' advocate she is today."

—Dennis N. Griffin, Retired NY Investigator, author, *Surviving The Mob: A Street Soldier's Life in the Gambino Crime Family*

"Raw and riveting *Holding My Hand Through Hell* starts fast and never lets up. In this powerful memoir, author Susan Murphy Milano throws open her personal closet so that we see what drives this woman to tirelessly champion voiceless victims and the people who love them."

—Steve Jackson, *NY Times* bestselling author, *Not Lost Forever*

Holding My Hand Through Hell

A Real Life Journey of Hope, Survival, Murder, and Abuse

Susan Murphy Milano

Ice Cube Press, LLC
North Liberty, Iowa

Holding My Hand Through Hell—
A Real Life Journey of Hope, Survival, Murder, and Abuse.

ISBN 9781888160673   1 3 5 7 9 8 6 4 2

Library of Congress Control Number: 2012931591

Ice Cube Press, LLC (Est. 1993)
www.icecubepress.com
steve@icecubepress.com

The paper used in this publication meets the minimum requirements of the American National Standard for Information Sciences—Permanence of Paper for Printed Library Materials, ANSI Z39.48-1992.

Manufactured in the United States of America with recycled paper

Author photo courtesy of Monica Caison, founder of the CUE Center for Missing persons, www.ncmissingpersons.org. Small inset photo on cover is of the author.

Dedication:

This book is dedicated to Peggy Bettis. Words don't seem to be enough in expressing how grateful I am for all your support and dedication. This book is because of you my dear friend, for teaching me if I imagined and believed, anything is possible!

Foreword
by Diane Fanning

Thirty years ago I would have never imagined I'd be the author of eleven true crime books and six mystery novels. But, of course, at that time, my dreams were overshadowed by a crushing lack of self-confidence. I was an abused woman, although I did not want to believe this at the time. My abuse was easy to deny because it was predominantly emotional—the physical abuse included shoves, arm grips that left bruises but nothing more. I told myself I was not a victim. I just needed to be a better person.

The turning point came when I got a new job after my daughter's birth. After my first day at work I cried all the way home because people were so nice to me. Listening to my first husband for twelve-and-a-half years of marriage had convinced me that I was not at all likeable.

Soon after, on an icy night, he cornered me in our loft bedroom, three stories from the ground. Fearing for my safety, I escaped into the bathroom and locked the door. The pounding and strident demands for entry escalated my terror and drove me out of the bathroom window, onto the icy roof. I crawled to the far corner, jumped down on a high snow bank then slipped and slid down the half-mile driveway to get away. It was a risky action but one of the best decisions I've ever made.

Still, I would not admit to myself—let alone anyone else—that I had been a victim of domestic abuse. Susan Murphy Milano changed all that. She opened her heart and understood the instinctive passion for victims she found in my books. Her acceptance and appreciation enabled me to look at the truth of my past, acknowledge it, and finally heal the scars I had so long denied.

For decades, Susan Murphy-Milano has been a tireless advocate for victims of domestic violence, the missing, and the dead. She has proactively pushed for the safety of women in bad relationships, writing *Time's Up*, the phenomenal handbook for anyone wanting to escape from a negative relationship. She created the unique *Evidentiary Abuse Affidavit*, a videotaped testimony recorded by the stalked, harassed, or abused victims to offer protection to them or at the very least, ensure that justice is served if their struggle for freedom turns fatal.

Throughout all her work, she has remained silent about the history of her own life—the incidents that gave birth to her passion for safety and justice—until now. In *Holding My Hand Through Hell*, Susan details the abusive environment created by her policeman father in her birth home. She reveals her own bad relationship decisions, and the journey that took her from victim to advocate.

Once I discovered the story of her life, I was even more impressed with Susan—she became one of my heroes. She is a testament to our ability as humans to take the worst moments of our lives and turn them into something positive. She has taken the hard-earned lessons from her life's rocky path and used them to help others.

Susan is a shining example to us all—an inspiration to do more and do it better than we ever have done before. *Holding my Hand Through Hell* is a dramatic and cautionary tale, a story of courage, and a wake-up call to our dormant hopes and dreams.

Susan brought me to a point of introspection where I could stop hiding from myself, embrace my past, and move forward stronger, more aware, and more compassionate. She has been an inspiration for Homicide Detective Lucinda Pierce, the lead character in five of my novels, whose worst memories mirror much of what happened in Susan's life.

Hold Susan's hand through this journey through hell. When you reach the other side, you'll be stronger, more grateful and imbued with a hope that will never die. *Holding My Hand Through Hell* is life-affirming and thought provoking—just like Susan.

—Diane Fanning

Diane Fanning is a best-selling *New York Times* true crime and non-fiction author. To learn more visit www.dianefanning.com

Chapter One
Silent Night
January 19, 1989

Unable to reach my mother, Roberta, by telephone, I grew anxious. Around 1 AM I drove to my mother's apartment, she was nowhere to be found. Returning to my car I drove the sixteen blocks to my childhood home where my father, Phillip, still lived since my parents had divorced.

Startled to see my mother's car parked in front of the three bedroom bungalow I slammed my foot down on the brake, threw the gear in park and with the car engine still running jumped out and bounded the five steps to the front door and rang the bell.

Receiving no response I moved to the rear of the house and climbed on top of the central air conditioning unit that was situated just below my father's bedroom. The curtains covering the window were too thick to peer through, but I could clearly hear the television blaring at full volume. Removing a shoe I pounded on the heavy storm window.

"Open the door! Let me in!" I screamed.

A neighbor I knew, startled awake by my screams, yelled across the yard that I was welcome to use the phone to call the police.

"No thanks, I can get in," I said, climbing down from the window.

Walking around to the side door, I noticed the glass had been broken and replaced with a heavy piece of plywood, now secured by fresh nails. I tossed my winter jacket on the sidewalk and tried to push the plywood in using my arms and body weight. Although I couldn't break through I was able to wedge my arm in far enough to undo the latch that held the door shut.

"Son of a bitch," I cursed. Pulling my arm back out the skin on my forearm had been torn open, catching one the nails. Taking off a shoe I removed one of my socks and tied it around the deep gash to stop the bleeding.

Holding my arm in pain, I cautiously stepped inside the entryway, onto the linoleum landing inside the house. The stifling air inside grabbed at my nostrils and I dropped down to my knees. The smell was overpowering and I feared associated with death.

I felt disoriented. Crawling on my hands and knees up the few short steps leading into the dark kitchen I tried to focus my eyes in the room. The heavy, foul odor got to me. I turned my head to the side and vomited.

If by nothing but sheer will, I forced myself to go on and investigate, inching my way across the kitchen floor on my knees, towards an object laying ahead of me. I almost immediately recognized it was a dead body. The feet, with shoes and socks pointed in my direction, had a familiar panda bear pattern on them. My mind was reeling, my worst fear realized. It was my mother, lying in a crusted pool of her own blood, dead. I rose up from the dark kitchen floor and bolted over to the neighbor's house for help.

"Please," I begged, "call 911 and tell them there is a body on the floor!"

The neighbor, Barbara, insisted I come into the house. Seeing that I was in shock and that my arm was bleeding she quickly grabbed a kitchen towel from a nearby drawer, put ice cubes in it and wrappedthe towel around my arm. I used the woman's phone to call 911.

"How do you know it's a body?" the operator asked.

My intense emotions from seeing the horror in my childhood home caused me to slam the phone down on the 911 operator and call the Area Five Violent Crimes and Homicide Unit direct. A detective answered on the second ring. On the verge of hysteria, I tried to calm my trembling, high-pitched, voice, "This is Detective Phil Murphy's daughter," I cried. "There's a body in my parents' house!"

"I'm sorry, could you repeat that?" he answered, cautiously.

Was nobody listening?

"A body!" I shouted. "A corpse! I don't know whose, but there's a body!"

"Where's your father?" the detective anxiously posed the question.

"I don't know! Please! Please send someone right away!"

With a promise to meet responding officers, I hung up the phone and my thoughts drifted to my car, still running in the middle of the street. Barbara said she would take care of it.

Within five minutes, emergency fire trucks, ambulances, and police cars roared onto the residential street. I was waiting for officers at the front door of my childhood home to direct them down the gangway to the rear of the house.

Officers, not knowing if a potential threat lurked inside, drew their weapons as they entered. I tried to follow, but was blocked by a heavy set police captain standing guard like a fierce mastiff.

"Don't even think about it," he growled.

Standing at the back door, I did my best to see over the captain's broad shoulders and into the kitchen. All I could see was that the pale, yellow kitchen wall and refrigerator were covered with blood. I felt compelled to get back inside the house.

The watch-dog captain, sensing my intentions, called two police officers over to him and instructed them to escort me back to the neighbor's house. As officers were walking me back, I dropped to my knees doubled over with stomach cramps on the cold concrete. "Oh, shit. I'm pregnant."

I heard one of the officers radio for another ambulance. "No, no I'm not going anywhere, help me up and take me next door. If I'm losing this baby there is nothing anyone can do about it," I said.

A female officer knelt down beside me, "how far along are you?"

I replied, "six weeks."

She pulled my hair away from my face, "let them take you in to be checked. I have an ambulance on the way for you." I shook my head no. When the cramps subsided I picked myself up and the officers followed behind carrying out their orders. I found myself at Barbara's again, facing the police department's chaplain, Father Nagel. Reaching out for my icy hands, he held them both gently, warming them, as he delivered the devastating news.

"I'm sorry to be the one telling you this, it's the worst part of my job," he said quietly, with great concern in his eyes, "but your mother has been murdered. I can tell you with certainty that your mother didn't suffer and likely had no warning what was about to happen. She was shot from behind, at close range." He continued delivering the horrific message. "Your father was in the bedroom. He also died, of a self-inflicted gunshot wound to the head."

Staring at Father Nagel, in shock and disbelief, I listened quietly as he told me what to expect. He asked if he could contact anyone for me. Lastly, he requested my permission to administer last rites to my parents.

Shortly afterwards, absorbing the reality of the night's events, I was approached by Detective Weber, the detective who had answered the phone that night. After expressing his deep condolences and taking my statement, he noticed my arm.

"Let's get one of the medics over here to look at this," he called out to his partner, but before the medic arrived, I noticed Detective Tom Flaherty walk through the front door. Off-duty, he had been called by a detective from within the unit, informing him there was an emergency at his partner's house and he should get over there to meet me.

Acknowledging Detective Weber with a nod, Detective Tom Flaherty, my father's partner for twenty years, sat down beside me, devastated. "Susan, I'm at a loss…this is terrible." His voice was low and with purpose, "Your father was like a brother to me, a great man. When you're finished with the medic and Detective Weber, have someone notify me and we'll talk."

About an hour later I found myself facing Detective Tom Flaherty again. This time my tone of voice and stoic nature demanded straight answers from my father's former partner. I wanted to know everything that had happened in the house. Motioning for me to sit down on Barbara's couch, Tom let out a loud, defeated, sigh.

"Phil had a lot to drink," he began, his red eyes showing the depths of his emotions. "It's difficult for me to discuss the details with you but your mother was found in the kitchen on the floor. She had been shot with a .44 Magnum. The bullet exited out her right eye and onto the kitchen table." Tom took a deep breath. "Looks like after he shot her Phil took a towel and covered her face. He was found in the bedroom and had shot himself. Susan, when was the last time you spoke with him?"

For reasons foreign to me, I felt enraged at the question.

"He murdered my mother! *Your* superhero partner murdered her and you want to know when I spoke to him last? You're just as cold and heartless as he was!" I stood up, knowing I wanted no part of the conversation.

"Susan, wait, calm down," Tom also stood. "I know you're upset but there's no reason to speak to *me* that way!"

I spun around to face him, a man I'd known since childhood. My face, showing the contempt I was feeling at that moment, made Tom Flaherty stop in his tracks.

"Bullshit!" I shouted, "all you care about is *your* buddy and how you can cover up his mess one more time!"

Knowing he had no defense against the spew of accusations, Detective Tom Flaherty hung his head in shame and left the residence. I stood motionless, staring at the door, wondering if I should scream or cry—or both. I was in shock, my ultimate fears realized. I felt a sense of relief when Father Nagel came back inside to speak with me, closing the door behind him as if to shield me from seeing the activity out front.

"They are preparing to transport the bodies to the morgue," he said in almost a whisper. "Someone from the department will call you in the morning to assist you with the funeral arrangements. Susan, is there anything I can do for you?" Blankly I stared at his face. Sensing my emotions, Father Nagel shifted his body as if he was blocking me from going outside.

"Please move away from the door, I'm going outside to watch," I told him. Father Nagel came out and stood beside me. From the neighbor's front stoop I watched as officers carried each body out on stretchers. They loaded my parents on opposite sides of a dirty, banged up paddy wagon for transport to the morgue.

I shook my head, surprised to feel the warmth of the single tear that ran down my cheek, a tear that had remained hidden—until now. Then, with the promise of being in touch soon, Father Nagel left my side.

I wasn't allowed to re-enter the house until sunrise. Most of the officers were gone by then. I felt a huge sense of apprehension as I walked through the same doorway I had entered hours before. With each step my legs and feet felt heavy. The strong smell of death remained in the air.

Tom Flaherty walked in behind me, desperate to redeem himself in the eyes of his partner's daughter. He wanted to ensure, in his own mind, that I would be okay.

As I stood in the doorway of my father's bedroom, I noticed the mattress that had recently held his lifeless body had been removed—a professional courtesy by the responding officers to the family.

The kitchen floor was caked with dried blood where my mother had fallen to her death after the gunshot—a shot that had been administered by my own father, her former husband. Even though they had been divorced, I knew my mother would never escape the wrath of my father. The blood stains I stared at proved this.

On the kitchen table was a large cassette recorder and the red record light was on. I pressed the eject button and put the cassette in my coat pocket. Flaherty caught me slipping something into my pocket, demanding to know what I took. He held out his palm and said, "hand it over."

"Go to hell," I snapped back, quickly turning to walk away.

Flaherty extended his arm, grabbing my shoulder and spun me around. In anger Flaherty raised his voice, "Who do you think you're talking too?" he demanded.

My voice cracked in response, "Leave me alone! Your partner murdered my mother."

A commander from the department walked into the house where we were arguing, asking what all the shouting was about? Flaherty lowered his head, "I'm sorry sir, Phil and I were so close, like brothers, I lost my temper. I apologize." He walked away to another part of the house.

The commander extended his condolences for my loss before asking me additional questions about my father.

"I'm sorry for having to ask you more questions, but did your father give you any indication he was planning on doing something like this?"

I clammed up, feeling it served no purpose in disclosing the fact I'd met my father for breakfast just days prior.

"Had your father been behaving in anyway out of the ordinary?"

I responded, "No."

"Susan, how did you know to come to the house?" asked the commander.

"When I couldn't reach my mom, I knew something was wrong."

"Yeah, but how? How did you know to come here?" I looked at the commander before responding, as if he was crazy for asking such a ridiculous question.

I thought to myself, how can it be? Not one of these officers is talking about what they always knew? The police department was the keeper of my father's dark secret. There was never any concern for my mother and her children while she alive. Then I said, "She's dead! From as far back as I can remember he'd always promised he'd kill her if she ever left him."

Before responding, the commander took a deep breath. "I'm sorry, I had to ask, part of my job." The commander took out a card from his wallet, gently placing it in my hand, "You need anything, you hear anything, get a hold of me."

When we finished I headed into the living room. I looked at the worn out recliner my father had lived and breathed in.

On the table next to the chair was an ashtray overflowing with cigarette butts, a bottle of cranberry juice, and an empty, half-gallon bottle of cheap vodka. Reaching under the chair, I found a loaded gun and my father's old black leather wallet. Inside the wallet was a note dated January 17, 1989. There was no signature, but it was clearly his handwriting. The note read: *To whom it may concern. This is business only. I did what I had to do. No one leaves me and gets away with it, so I'm taking care of business.*

Chapter Two
No More Sweet Dreams

It was late when I heard keys opening the front door. Clutching my doll Molly I pretended to be asleep. Closing my eyes tight as the familiar sound of the heavy shoes walked past my bedroom door. I said a silent prayer, "God, please protect my mommy." Without seeing my father, I knew he was drunk.

My bedroom was next to my parents. I heard my father flip on the light switch in their bedroom. Slurring his words, "Roberta get up, now! I'm hungry make me something. Roberta, come on! Get your ass out of bed!"

I gripped a hold of my doll even tighter as if she could protect and comfort me.

The heated words lasted a few minutes before my mother responded by getting out of bed to go and check in on my younger brother Bobby, then me.

After my father ate, they shut the door and went to bed. Through the walls I could hear my parents talking. My father's voice went from a drunken calm to an angry tone. I didn't need a magic crystal ball to predict what would happen next.

The sound of breaking glass crashed to the bare bedroom floor, piercing the silence of the night.

"Phil, get to sleep and leave me alone," my mother said.

I could hear, from the tone in his angry voice, all hell was was about to explode. Curled in a fetal position up against my bedroom wall, I whispered, "Please God, make Daddy stop, I will be good, I promise."

"Phillip, don't! Stop! Please you're hurting me." It sounded as if he'd thrown her out of bed and onto the floor. My younger brother Bobby came into my bed, trembling as he climbed under the covers, "Susie, I'm scared,"

Bobby's voice quivered. I tucked him under the covers and told him to stay put in bed.

I ran into my parents' room. My father in his white t-shirt and underwear had my mother pinned down on the floor next to their bed. On the floor were jagged pieces of shattered glass. Blood was running down the side of my mother's head. My father, with his hands on her neck was smashing my mother's head against the metal iron bed railing, shouting, "Why don't you listen to me? Why can't you do as you're told, Roberta?"

Bobby had jumped out of bed and stood next to me.

We were screaming for him to stop.

"Daddy, stop! Stop hurting Mommy!" we cried.

"Son of a bitch," yelled my father. "Both of you go back to bed, now!"

My father continued to yell at my mother, "Bitch!" he shouted, "you're worthless!"

I was four years old, unable to fully grasp what was happening.

My father, a decorated Chicago police detective in my eyes, was nothing more, nothing less than a monster. Night after night he terrorized his own flesh and blood.

I didn't love my father, I feared him. My father was incapable of loving. Most nights I stood by helplessly, watching my father physically abuse my mother.

The sound of the heavy slaps sent a deep jolt through my body.

I'd try to get my brother back into bed.

My mother would yell at me, "Leave the bedroom, baby. Get out."

I'd scream.

She'd yell again, "Go on, honey. Back to bed, now!"

One time, I dragged a kitchen chair directly under the telephone. Next to the spice rack was a pencil. I used it to dial the rotary phone in the kitchen placing a call to the operator to send someone to help us.

When the operator's voice answered I yelled, "Help," dropping the phone. I watched the receiver as it swung back and forth from its cord as if it were hands on a grandfather clock. I went back to their room.

My eyes widened in horror. My knees trembled at the thought he was about to kill her.

On the bedroom floor my parents wrestled with the gun.

"Stop, stop! Mommy, be careful!" I cried.

Bang!

The gun went off. I thought my mom was shot and dying.

Distraught, I ran out of the bedroom, jumped on a step stool, pulled the metal chain off from the front door, and in my night-gown and bare feet, ran out on the front yard, screaming at the top of my lungs.

"Help me! Please, help me! " I cried, pleading for anyone within ear shot to rescue us.

My father came from behind and scooped me up, carrying me. I kicked and screamed to let me go. "Calm down! It's okay, shush, calm down…shush."

I jumped out of my father's arms and ran into the bedroom. My mother was bleeding from her head, crying, and curled up like a ball in the corner.

My mom's face was quickly swelling in size as a result of the beating.

"Everything's fine, baby," said my mother, pointing to the floor. "The bullet went into the floor near the vent. It's okay. No one got hurt.

I cried, "Mommy, you're hurt. Mommy, you're bleeding!"

"Mommy and Daddy were just arguing. I'm fine, honey. You know Mommy and Daddy love you very much."

Mom took me to my room. Gently tucking my doll Molly in my arms assuring me everything was going to be alright.

My dad packed a few days of work clothes and left. He came home three days later and behaved as if nothing happened. Mom remained silent.

My brother Bobby and I were confused. We internalized at some level that my parents fought because we did something wrong. It was a feeling you couldn't describe, you just felt it to be true. Sometimes I'd think if I wasn't born, they would have nothing to argue and fight about.

My life was bewildering. When we watched television shows like *Ozzie and Harriet* or *Leave it to Beaver* we noticed these families never quarreled. My brother and I made a pact—we were going to keep our rooms clean, pick up our toys, obey our parents, and like magic, we would become a happy family, just like the ones we watched on television.

As children, we also said our prayers every night.

I prayed to God to make my mommy and daddy stop fighting.

The more I prayed though the more my parents seemed to fight.

I just didn't understand. I thought if you are good, God watches and protects you and makes everything good in your life.

But, when you do something bad, God will send you straight into hell.

I relied on a cartoon-like caricature for my mental picture of the devil. Wearing a bright red, fire-proof suit, with pointy cone shaped horns popping out of his head, black fuzzy sideburns with a beard, and holding a sharp pitch fork.

I believed that God sent bad people into the hot dungeon of hell, chained to a large railing, to live for all eternity.

As small child, the mere thought of this place was frightening.

Each time I would hear a grown-up say, "You know if you tell a lie and don't go to confession, or if you steal something without paying for it, you're going straight to hell." If I did anything wrong,

I was always told, "God will punish you and you're going to hell without your dolls and toys."

A couple of years passed and despite continuing to feel helpless, praying, and asking God to help me and my family, God didn't answer me back. I witnessed no miracle. I began to believe that God was an imaginary character invented by parents just like Santa Claus at Christmas time.

One thing was for certain though, I was scared of my father. Sometimes when I was supposed to be sleeping, I could hear my father shout at my mother, "Who's going to believe *you*? I'm a policeman, I'll have you locked up, Roberta, and you'll never see your children again. If you even think of leaving me, I'll kill you and the kids, set the house on fire and get away with it."

When my father started talking about killing us I was even more scared. I had such terrible nightmares I'd even wet the bed sometimes.

I fully believed the day would come when I would die. I imagined my father killing my mother first, then coming into my bedroom and suffocating me to death with a pillow. Then he would walk down to Bobby's room and kill him with his pillow.

After we were all dead I imagined my father would get the big red gas can he kept in the tool shed, come back into the house and spread gasoline in front of each bedroom door. He would reach into his pocket for a packet of wooden matches, strike a flame, throw it onto the gasoline and leave us to burn. No one would ever suspect anything. He was a cop.

In the mid 1960s, there were no shelters for battered women. No one ever dared discuss their personal problems with others like we do today.

Family issues and problems were left to physicians in general practice from whom women like my mother received monthly prescriptions for valium to deal with the stress and pain in their lives. I chose to deal with the mental torture and abuse by using my mind as an imaginary playground.

If I was at a friend's house and saw how kind a father was to his kids I would imagine my life with that person's daddy, pretending to be happy. Or I'd imagine sitting down to a family meal where everyone asked about your day and how it was going.

As a child, one of my favorite television shows was *Bewitched*. I was fascinated by Elizabeth Montgomery's character's power to twitch her nose or snap her finger and make people vanish. Sometimes I would pretend I had the same powers and was able to make my father vanish to someplace like the North Pole. (It was the only place I could think up where my father would have no access to a car or a train. Thus, unable to return home.)

I often imagined my father being killed at work in some heroic fashion. Maybe gunned down during a heated gun battle with a bank robber.

My imagination would continue. Within hours a police department official would be dispatched to our home, ring the doorbell, and give my mother the news, my father had been killed. Secretly, I wished for the day my father would never again step foot through our front door again.

I was consumed with ways my father would magically disappear from our lives. My mind was the only thing my father had no control over. I learned how to use my mind as a playground, a safe place to escape.

Being from a police family had a lot of drawbacks, in addition to making sure I stayed out of trouble, everyone in the neighborhood and at school was under the impression my father was some sort of superhero. My father had special social status as a cop. He was seen by the world as a perfect father, provider, and police officer. He was the first to help a neighbor in distress. And the last person any would suspect of terrorizing his family.

Strangers would often comment and say what a lucky little girl I was to have such a wonderful father. I was expected to suck up the accolades, nod in agreement with strangers and say, "thank you."

For me to even attempt to make allegations of fear or violence against my father, the superhero crime fighter, caused school administrators and others to question my own mental stability.

My morning ritual, before climbing out of my bed, was to close my eyes tightly and say to myself, "Please make Mommy be here."

More than anything in the world, I needed my mom to be okay. In the mornings I wanted to see my mom in the kitchen preparing our lunches for school, but sometimes she was not in the house. Instead, Bobby and I would be greeted by Grandma Carolyn, my dad's mother, because my father had taken my mom to the hospital in the middle of the night for injuries sustained from his beatings.

I loved my grandmother, and often I wondered how such a sweet woman could have given birth to such an evil man. A devil with a badge.

As a child, Grandma Carolyn had contracted scarlet fever, permanently losing her hearing. Grandma Carolyn communicated by using her hands. I was taught sign language by my Grandmother so I could communicate with her. There were many times I wished she could hear her angry son, my father, as he terrorized us.

If I attempted to write down what I wanted to say to Grandma, she would ignore me, insisting I use sign language to communicate with her.

In the early days of television the sets didn't come with remote controls. You had to physically turn the television set on and off with your fingers, this made it difficult when we wanted to change the channel or turn up the volume. Grandma would stomp her foot on the carpet when my brother or I would get up and go near the television.

My grandmother taught herself to read people's lips on the television. I learned to read lips and use only sign language when she was at our house too.

In her late fifties, Grandma was a tall, attractive, grey haired, religious woman, a devout Catholic. Every morning after her two-mile walk she would make herself a cup of tea and prepare to go to morning mass.

Grandma kept her rosary beads on top of the Bible next to her bed and a pair of white gloves and a scarf neatly placed underneath in the dresser drawer. Sometimes I wanted to ask Grandma why she went to church but I was too afraid my question would come out wrong and get lost in my attempt to explain myself using sign language. I never saw anything but a great big smile on Grandma's face. Maybe that's why people called her, "sunshine."

She was happy and cheerful and she treated everyone with kindness. When I would go to the store with her and a cashier mumbled the amount due, I would use sign language to translate for my grandmother.

Sometimes I would hear strangers making cruel remarks. They would call her a "dummy" behind her back. From being out with my grandmother I learned that people are ignorant, reacting to their own fears.

Strangers didn't understand. My grandmother was very intelligent. Besides finishing the weekly crossword puzzle in the Sunday *New York Times* each week, my grandma had heightened senses beyond those of the hearing world. To me she was Super Grandma with magical gifts. Although she lived in a silent world, God allowed her to see in a way the hearing world would never understand.

Going to school was painful for me. I was not the brightest light bulb in the classroom. Most days I was too tired to pay attention in class due to the battles and drunken rages of my father.

I was confused and lonely. I didn't have many friends. I was unable to invite anyone over after school because I never knew what to expect. Sometimes my father would just be walking in from a night of drinking when I was returning home from school. And my mother's housekeeping skills were not the best. Our lives were as chaotic as the house. Laundry baskets were piled with clothes. Dishes always sat in the sink. The house was an honest reflection of our turbulent lives.

We had no structure in our home. Our daily routine was about how to survive and stay alive. Bobby, a year younger than me, was a skinny, blond haired boy with blue eyes. My father often remarked that mom must have had an affair with the milkman, questioning my mother and claiming he didn't believe Bobby was his own son.

As a result of my father's attitude he didn't have a healthy relationship with Bobby.

Bobby was sickly as a child. I often thought this had a lot to do with our environment. I never witnessed a warm moment, or even a simple word of praise for good grades on a report card. I think Bobby wanted to be close to my father, but the opportunity never presented itself.

Bobby loved baseball. He lived and breathed the sport. Dad never displayed any enthusiasm for Bobby's passion.

At the end of his second season of Little League, Bobby was named player-of-the-year in his division. A big banquet with awards was held at the park club house where they played. Bobby asked Dad to attend, and Dad agreed, but he didn't end up taking him, instead he made up some excuse about why he was not able to go. Bobby was devastated. He was the only kid at the banquet without his father in attendance.

In the third grade my mother enrolled me in Catholic religious classes. I was not thrilled. I would have rather gone to the dentist than attend classes required to make my first communion. Maybe

I wouldn't have felt that way if it was explained to me why I had to attend. But it was an order handed down by my father like a warden to his prisoner. "You will go," end of discussion.

As I entered my first religious class, we were greeted by a nun who shouted at the class while we took our seats. The nun was hard of hearing and didn't seem very fond of children. I wanted to slip out the side door of the classroom. The nun instructed the class to bow their heads in prayer. I stared off into space at the back of the classroom. The nun came up behind me and swatted the back of my neck with a long wooden ruler. "Ouch! That hurt," I exclaimed.

"It was supposed to hurt. Bow that head. Now!" she barked.

"No! I don't believe in God." I replied.

The nun picked me up by the hair, marched me out of the class-room, directly to the principal's office. She slammed me into a vacant seat, ordering me to stay put while she went into the principal's office.

A nun in a long black robe, with a large set of door keys affixed to her waist, appeared in the doorway and motioned me to enter the office. She had my file on her desk.

I went to sit down in the chair. The principal snapped her fingers at me, declaring, "I did not give you permission to sit."

I stood, as if I had committed a terrible crime.

"What's this I hear? You would not bow your head in prayer? You do not believe in God? Why are you here if you don't believe in God? All children who do not believe in God end up in hell! What do you have to say for yourself?"

I just looked at her thinking there's that place called hell again. I wanted to challenge the nun and ask that she show me this place in a photo, or somehow prove to me hell existed. Instead I stared at her for what seemed to be a long time before answering, "God doesn't answer my prayers. I pray for him to help us, and he doesn't listen."

The nun pursed her lips together.

"What do you pray to God about?"

"That my dad will stop beating my mom and stop hurting us," I replied.

"If this is some sort of joke, I'm not laughing. I know your family. Your father and I grew up just down the street from each other. You, child, are a liar," she declared.

The nun scanned the file in front of her and placed her index finger in the rotary telephone and dialed. My mother answered. I heard one side of the conversation, and it was not favorable. A half hour later my mother arrived. I was ordered out of the office while my mother and the nun spoke.

Mother came out, gently reached down, took hold of my hand and we headed for home. My father didn't allow my mother to take driving lessons and get her license. This was another way he controlled her life. My mother was forced to either walk everywhere or take the bus.

After a couple blocks, my mom finally spoke. "You know, honey, people don't understand. We can't tell anyone that Daddy hurts me or hits you. Do you understand?"

I nodded my head, yes, but I didn't mean it. I didn't understand. We stopped before crossing the busy intersection and mom bent down and spoke.

"Susan, this is our secret. We can't ever tell anyone what Daddy does. You and I both know, but people will think you're lying when you tell them. I know you may not understand right now, but someday, when you're all grown up and have a family of your own, you will. We must not breathe a word of this to your father, he will be angry. It's our little secret."

I didn't return for the next twelve sessions of religious class. They refunded the money by mail with a letter stating not to re-apply.

I was curious, and often wondered if all families kept secrets? There was no way I could ask or even talk with anyone. I didn't want to be embarrassed. I tried not to think about my problems.

The little girl with bright brown button eyes lived and played in her own private hell. My thoughts became my private playground.

Chapter Three
Open Invitation

In fourth grade, I was teamed up with a new kid in school named Tim on a science project. Tim's father was the new pastor at the Baptist church, not far from the elementary school.

After school, I followed Tim home to his house located behind the church, where he and his family lived.

Tim's mother was a beautiful woman with a warm friendly smile. She reminded me of the energetic and funny character of Laura, played by Mary Tyler Moore on the *Dick Van Dyke Show*. A popular television series in the mid 1960s.

Tim's mom wore a skirt, her dark hair was always combed back in a tight, perfect bun, and she wore bright red lipstick.

I enjoyed going to Tim's house, his mom always made a snack for us before we worked on our science project. From the moment I entered the front door of their home, I could sense the invisible layer of warmth and love. I felt safe.

The science and art fairs were big events. The school combined the evening with parent/teacher conferences. My father always worked nights at the police department, so he was never able to get off from work. My mom attended school events alone.

When the big day arrived Tim and I proudly displayed our electric erupting volcano. Parents and teachers walked around to all the displays in the gymnasium. I noticed my mother was not as nicely dressed as the other parents. She was wearing her signature white bobby socks and some type of smock dress that covered her pear-shaped body. I was embarrassed by her appearance for the first time in my life. I was keenly aware of the stares of other parents in the room as my mother walked around the gymnasium.

From across the brightly lit room I could see that my mother wore a headband using extra bobby pins in an attempt to mask certain sections of her hair that had been pulled out by my father. In fits of rage he would drag her by the top of the hair and pull her around the house.

I was hurt and confused by the reactions from parents and teachers. Hurt because my mother was my world. Confused about what I could do to make things better.

Beaming with a bright smile, my mother walked over to our science project exhibit. A large, rather tall man dressed in a suit also approached our booth.

"Hello, Dad!" said Tim.

"Son, what do we have here?" the man replied.

Tim explained, then without missing a beat, the man spun around and introduced himself to my mom.

The pastor bent his knees a bit, extending his very large hand to me. It wasn't often a grown-up treated me with kindness. His large hand was soft, radiating warmth.

"I'm Pastor Dunne. You must be Susan. It's very nice to meet you."

He resembled the holy look of the actor Victor Mature from the movies I watched with my mother.

Mother and the pastor began talking. I overheard the pastor inquire where our family attended church.

"We wouldn't be able to do that," mother replied. "We are Catholic. My husband would never approve."

"Mrs. Murphy, our weekly youth program is a nice way for the children to participate in activities. We don't change their faith. You think about. It's an open invitation." They laughed and he excused himself.

I sensed the pastor knew our family secret by the way Pastor Dunne spoke to my mother. He wasn't bossy or disrespectful. My mother was not told what to do. Pastor Dunne was merely extending an invitation.

On the way home, it was all I talked about.

"Please," I begged. "Can I go to the church?" All she would say was, "We'll see."

Several weeks later we bumped into the pastor at the neighborhood drug store.

"Glad to see you," said Pastor Dunne. My mom was uncomfortable, tugging at her clothes in an effort to hide the large black and blue bruises on her forearms. The pastor didn't say anything other than to remind her of the invitation for us to participate in activities at the church.

A few weeks later, Bobby and I were allowed to go, but the catch was we had to come right home and were sworn to secrecy. We were not to say anything to our father. He was against anything faith based unless it had something to do with the Catholic Church.

My father didn't have a high opinion of other religious groups. This included people of color. I would often hear my father refer to people he arrested as porch monkeys or niggers. And when he was especially angry with my mother he would call her a, "dumb nigger."

Saturdays, after watching cartoons and eating Froot Loops, Bobby and me went to the church. Sometimes we would learn songs from the Bible, or we would play games and win silly prizes. Of all the church activities I enjoyed working on art projects the most. The church supplied art materials and we would make things to bring home. My favorite was a stencil of my hands together on a piece of wood. I used lilac stones around the outside, and cream stones covered the hands in the picture. It looked like praying hands.

It was beautiful and my mother was so proud when I brought it home she put it on display on a wall in the hallway. It was the first time something I made with my hands hung in the house.

On Saturday evenings the Baptist Church hosted a pot luck dinner. Sometimes my mom would surprise us and show up with a home-baked dish. We stayed and ate with church members and their families. My mother was happy making small talk with other parents.

Watching her interact with others, I realized our lives were directly related to my father's moods. My father only cared about control. He would never take the time to know and love my mother. It was much easier for him to keep her cloaked in fear and isolation.

Whenever I thought about how my father treated my mother, I would get upset. At nine years old I knew what it meant to live with a man where our daily existence was literally held in the hands of uncertainty. And we were powerless to do anything about it.

Our home environment was toxic. With each passing year, it became more difficult to breathe the air in our home without choking. My father's angry rants increased, mainly over issues of little or no significance. If my mother didn't have his socks matched, or if his handkerchiefs were not folded properly, he threw a fit. If his breakfast eggs were too runny, he threw the plate across the kitchen, as though it was a Frisbee.

Most days, my father didn't return home from work until 4:00 AM. He almost always expected my mother to pop out of bed like a robot and wait on him. He purposely picked fights that only he could win. When Dad was off from work, he maintained strict control over my brother and me. We could not go out and play. Instead, when he was home, we remained in our rooms like prisoners confined in jail cells.

When he was home, there was no interaction as a family. We didn't talk about our day. Plans to do anything as a family never materialized. Something always came up or my father would make some excuse. If the circus was in town and my brother and me asked if we could go, my father said no. Once he gave his answer to any question we asked, Bobby and I knew never to ask him a second time, or we would suffer severe consequences.

My father drank vodka. He consumed a lot of it. The vodka smelled similar to the rubbing alcohol in the medicine chest. I could not comprehend the attraction to drinking anything with such a foul odor, and in fact, for years, I believed vodka was made from the same ingredients used in rubbing alcohol.

Trips to the emergency room were common. My father would coach my mother on what to say once we arrived at the hospital, especially when the beatings she sustained resulted in a broken bone or two. With greater frequency, my mother was admitted to the hospital for extended periods of time, recovering from broken bones or internal injuries as a result of my father's abuse.

One afternoon after school I took the bus to visit my mother in the hospital. When I arrived in the hospital room her doctor was waiting for my mother to come out of the bathroom. When the doctor said hello he touched my shoulder. His jacket sleeve rose up and I could see a number tattooed on his arm. I asked what it meant. In a thick German accent, the doctor said it was what the Germans did to all the Jewish prisoners in the concentration camps during the war. "They tattooed all the Jews with numbers. Beaten women like your mother have a different tattoo, one that is not visible to the human eye, because it's on the inside."

"You know?" I asked.

"Yes, and like I have told your mother before, she has to leave before your father kills her. Tell your mother I'll stop back in later."

I didn't know what to make of the conversation with the doctor. I believed that admitting her into the hospital so often was the doctor's way of keeping my mother safe, both mentally and physically.

One afternoon my mom told Bobby and me that from now on we were to shout out to her from the gangway when we came home from school. If she didn't answer, we were not allowed to enter the house. "If I don't answer, I need you to run to the last house down the street, and say your mom is hurt, and ask them to please call for help. Under no circumstances are you to come inside and look for me. This is important," she instructed us.

For a few weeks, she had us practice, like a fire drill. My mom didn't want us to come home and find her dead body someplace in the house. She didn't use the word dead, but instinctively I knew what my mother meant.

Around the age of eleven my mom began confiding to me her plans to leave my dad once and for all. I was relieved. Maybe God did exist? Perhaps he was hearing and seeing the hell in which we were living.

One day I asked my mother if I could go to the Baptist Church on Sundays. I wanted to go to Bible school. I was interested in learning about God. My mother gave me permission as long as my dad didn't find out. I could not put it into words, but I knew people who went to church seemed happy. Perhaps the people in attendance at church were happy because they loved and cared about one another. I looked for marks and bruises on the women in church. I didn't see any. I saw fathers gently holding the hands of their children. I saw another man happily bounce a toddler on his knee. I longed for that warmth. The love of a father was something I could only witness, like a spectator watching images on a movie screen.

After church I attended Sunday school. A short, stocky, bald man with overgrown bushy eyebrows and hairs growing out of his noise presided over class. He illustrated Bible stories by using props and costumes, he made certain our experience during Sunday school was memorable. Sometimes he would call upon me to help him, even if, at times, I didn't fully understand the meaning of his stories. The Sunday school teacher talked at length how Jesus died on the cross for our sins, and if we accepted Jesus as our Lord and Savior, we would join God in his kingdom after we died.

I was confused, wondering how a man so important could die long ago for our sins now. I was taught that before we are admitted into heaven, we must accept Jesus into our hearts. God wanted people to be saved. So he sacrificed his Son to set us free.

As a child it sounded like a made up story by another grown-up, yet somehow I must have believed Jesus died for sins, because, I was eager to learn more. I wanted to understand what it meant to be saved. I had no intention of going to hell, and in the Baptist Church I learned no matter what sins you commit, if you take Christ into your heart, God will forgive and wipe away your sins like an eraser on a chalkboard.

One day, after dad left for work, mother announced we were leaving in the morning. She told Bobby and me to pick our favorite toy and one book.

We were limited to what we could take with us on the trip. I was happy. I didn't ask where we were going. All that mattered was that we were leaving. My mom said, "we're beginning a new adventure."

More importantly, I knew instinctively, and by her tone of voice, we would never be afraid again.

That night, before going to sleep, I said a prayer of thanks to God. It was more like a conversation with my hands folded together. "Please keep us safe on our adventure. I'm really happy you're helping my mother. I'll talk to you again soon. Amen. Oh, I forgot, one more thing, I promise to say my prayers nightly."

Early the following morning, as our father slept, we took the suitcases and left for the bus station.

It was our first time in a bus terminal. Crowds of people of all sizes, shapes, and colors filled the waiting areas. Mom went to a counter and purchased bus tickets. At the window, she was told the bus would be delayed for two hours. She didn't seem to care.

My mom held onto the tickets as if she won the lottery jackpot.

We sat closest to a boarding gate marked, "Ohio."

Bobby and I played a game of checkers as we waited to board the bus.

Finally, when it was time, we dragged our heavy suitcases out onto a concrete platform. A porter took our luggage and carried it to a storage compartment located at the back of the bus.

We boarded with others I imagined to be escaping from something horrible too. I scanned the faces of each passenger boarding the bus. Some passengers looked sad. Others, I assumed, were running away from home like us. My mother tapped my knee and asked me to, "stop staring at people, it wasn't polite."

Bobby and I shared a window seat with Mom across the aisle from us.

The bus driver started the engine. Over the intercom, the driver announced our destination and a travel time of six hours. The bus pulled out of the terminal and we were on our way.

Ten minutes after leaving the bus station, the bus driver took a call over the radio. He got on the intercom informing all of us that we were stopping for about ten minutes.

Mom didn't pay any attention, until we heard the driver open the door to the bus. Up the stairs of the bus came my father. I watched in terror as he flashed his badge to the driver walking down the aisle, past each row of passengers. He was coming to get his prisoners.

Mom gasped, "Oh my God! It's your father!" In fear, Bobby looked over at me and grabbed onto my hand. "Oh no, Susie, what are we gonna do?" He whispered. We sat frozen with fear in the seats.

"Come on, Roberta. Get up. Now!" he said.

The bus driver got off, went to the back of the bus, opened the compartment and handed our father the suitcases. I wanted to cry but under the circumstances I knew it was not a good idea.

My head was racing trying to figure out how my father found us, how he knew what bus we were on. All the way home my father ranted in the car. Bobby stayed quiet, keeping his head down, nervously pulling his hair.

"You think I'm an idiot, that I wouldn't be able to find you? Dummy up, Roberta. I find people and solve crime for a living." He was holding the back of her head, shaking it while he was driving. "What did I tell you? You'll never be able to leave me alive."

At that moment I thought about God. How could God let me down? We were so close to freedom? I blamed myself. I knew I was the reason my parents had to get married and, so I believed, everything was all my fault.

My parents had met at a drive-in restaurant called Skips on North Avenue in Chicago. My mother, Roberta, was just 17 years old. My father, Phil, was 24 years of age.

Both my father's parents were deaf before they were toddlers, as a result of childhood diseases. My father's parents communicated by using sign language.

My father stood over six feet tall. When he entered a room, everyone turned around. His commanding presence was like thunder rolling through a room. My mother was quite a bit shorter at five feet two inches. She was a brown eyed, well-endowed teenager with deep set European eyes and an infectious laugh.

My mother's parents were Russian Jews who lived a strict kosher life. They were angry when my mother informed them she was pregnant by an Irish Catholic man who, in their eyes, was too old for their daughter. As a child, my mother only told me bits and pieces about their rocky courtship and marriage. And she always made sure to tell me I was her pride and joy.

Regardless, my mother loved my father. Not once did she ever speak in an angry or mean tone about him. No matter how my father treated her, she continued to love him. This was very frustrating and confusing to me.

My parents were like oil and water. Phillip was strict. He managed to keep tabs on his wife to the point of obsession. If he called the house from work and my mother didn't answer, he would later interrogate her, demanding to know where she had been and with whom.

My mother was the last person anyone would suspect of having an affair. She was not an attractive woman. Her weight was a constant issue and she was as round as she was tall. Her love of food and anything sweet were her constant companions. She was an excellent cook who wore most of what she ate on her hips. Her most important qualities were her sincere warmth and deep love for her children.

My father was a different story with his children. He failed to communicate on a loving level. He was a strict commander of his domain. When he spoke, he expected everyone to jump. Often my father would say to Bobby and me, "Little children should be seen and not heard," followed with a raise of his left eyebrow and the words, "Do I make myself clear?" When Bobby or I didn't obey, my father used a belt to punish us.

In contrast, every day my mother told us, and me in particular, how important we were to her and how much she loved us. We could feel this in the air when our father was out of the house. She was like a soft, warm blanket surrounding us. She tried to instill values of love and hope in both Bobby and me.

Ironically, she was not capable of defending or loving herself enough to leave her abusive, and dangerous husband. My mother never came out and said it, but by her actions it was clear that she feared my father.

As my father drove his family home from the bus, I could see in the rear view mirror the anger building in his face. My stomach was in knots.

Chapter Four
Running Away From Home

The moment he put his key in the front door, Dad instructed my brother and me to go directly to our rooms. My father walked to each bedroom door, locking Bobby and me inside our rooms.

"Do not come out. Do you understand me?"

"Yes, sir," we replied, but I paced back and forth in my bedroom, thinking. I looked at my dolls, sitting on the bed with their eyes opened. If only they could come to life and help me with a plan to unlock the door. It was no use, I was locked in. There was no way I could get the door open.

I wondered all sorts of things, "What if he killed my mother and then came after us? What would I do? What if he sets the house on fire? How will I escape?"

"Please God," I said, "if you can hear me, help us."

The window to my bedroom was locked. A double set of storm windows made of an unbreakable material made it virtually impossible to open the window and climb out. Using my bed I jumped up in the air trying to get a better look at the window. In between the inside window and the storm window, I saw what appeared to be a screwdriver. My father must have forgotten about it.

The window and ledge seemed so high and out of my reach. Quickly, I emptied out the toys from a toy box on the floor. I pushed the wooden box over to the wall directly under the window and climbed on top.

I reached into the window ledge and got the screwdriver. My heart was racing. I kept thinking my father was going to come into my room next and kill me. In my mind his words to my mother about burning down the house played over and over like a broken record.

I heard screams from the bedroom. They pierced my heart. I worked quickly to unscrew the inside window. Next, I undid the screws holding the storm window in its track to the outside.

Once the storm window was loose it fell from its tracks dropping to the ground. With every ounce of strength I managed to pull myself up to the bedroom window. It was a long drop to the ground.

I was scared. I took out the big blue blanket from my closet and tossed it out the window, then stripped my bed pillows and bedding, pushing the soft material out the window. With my eyes closed I jumped onto the pile of blankets and pillows.

After my safe landing, I ran to the front door. It was locked, as was the side door in the gangway. In the back yard I climbed on top of the large central air conditioning unit. I couldn't see anything through the heavy curtains.

My mother screamed for somebody to help. I sat down for a moment to think. I had no way of getting back inside the house. Then, the idea came to me! In the tool shed my father always kept a full can of gasoline for the lawnmower. In the middle of the yard, I dragged patio furniture, wood, old rags and whatever else I could find that would burn. I emptied the full can of gas on the items I'd collected. Next I searched for matches. I could not find any. Remembering my father never locked his car, I rummaged around the front seat for a pack of matches, which I found on the floor. I headed back to the back yard, lit the entire pack of matches to an old rag, and threw it onto the pile. Success! It ignited.

I ran about two blocks from our house to the drugstore and asked the clerk behind the counter if I could use the phone. With his arms folded across his chest, he hesitated for a moment.

"It's an emergency! Please!"

I dialed the operator.

"Yes, I need help. It's a fire. Please send an ambulance and a fire truck to 710 W. Highland, Avenue. Hurry!"

I ran back to the house. I was proud of myself for thinking up a successful plan. I knew I would be in big trouble once my father learned I'd sneaked out from my room. I wasn't afraid.

Within a few minutes the jumbo red fire trucks came barreling down the residential street. At street level, you could see the smoke and flames shooting from the back of the house. The firemen ran to the backyard with their hoses. Within moments of the firemen working on extinguishing the fire, my father ran out of the house. His white t-shirt was covered with bright red blood.

"Mommy, Mommy," I screamed as I re-entered the house. She was lying unconscious on the bedroom floor. Her face was swollen, beaten beyond recognition.

I ran back outside to get help.

"My mother, my mother, she needs help. She's not moving!"

One of the firemen ran into the house and yelled for help. "We need a stretcher, on the double." They stabilized my mother before moving her onto a stretcher and into the back of the ambulance that looked more like a hearse.

I remembered my brother was still locked in his bedroom. I didn't have a key. I went to the hall closet and grabbed a metal coat hanger. I bent the end straight and jiggled it in the door knob. After several attempts the door lock popped open and I was able to gain entry. Bobby was crying and I quieted him down as we headed outside.

The neighbors on the block gathered to see what was going on.

A fireman stood nearby watching Bobby and me.

My father was laughing it up with one of the police officers as he walked out to the front of the house.

"What's wrong with these people?" I thought. "Why are they ignoring my mother's blood on his t-shirt? How come he's not being arrested?"

It seemed invisible to everyone.

It infuriated me to watch people treat my father like he was some sort of royalty.

My father walked over to where Bobby and me were standing and it was clear he was angry as he approached us. The look on his face meant I was in big trouble.

The fireman immediately intervened. Standing in the middle of me and my father, the firefighter extended his hand out to my father.

"Hey, they took your wife to the hospital. Maybe you should go and see if she's going to be alright, the kids can stay here with one of the neighbors…"

The neighbor two doors down offered to watch Bobby and me for the night.

"You go ahead, Phil. Go to the hospital. I'll make sure the kids are fed and put to bed early. Don't worry."

My father tightened his lips as he thanked the neighbor for her kindness.

Before he left, he motioned for me to walk over to him.

"You're not going to walk for a week when I finish with you. I told you to stay in your room. I'll deal with you later."

The next day Bobby and I rode with the neighbor to check on my mom in the hospital.

They didn't allow children under twelve into a patient's room, however, the neighbor worked at the hospital and she was able to get us in to visit with our mother for a few minutes. Mom's leg was broken and in a cast. She had some internal injuries. Her face looked like a train wreck. Both eyes were beaten shut. The neighbor assured Roberta she would take care of Bobby and me until she was released from the hospital.

My mother asked to speak with me alone, so the neighbor and Bobby left.

"Come up close to the bed. I can't see very well."

I drew near to her bed. "Susie, did you do what I think you did?"

With my head down in shame, "Yes, Mommy," I replied.

"My brave warrior girl. I'm not mad at you. The man who brought me here in the ambulance told me the fireman found me in the house. You started the fire, and I know you did it to help me, but you could have gotten hurt. My brave firecracker, Mommy is very proud of you. Susie I know you won't understand this now— someday, Honey, your bravery will be very important to who you become as a person. Stay clear of your father if you can until I come home. Watch over your brother and no fighting. Be on your best behavior while you're at Mrs. Abbott's home. I love you, Susie."

"Okay, Mommy, I love you too."

My father was missing in action. When we returned from the hospital to the neighbors, my father had left a note taped to her front door saying he had to go out of town on police business. He would be gone for several days.

Happily, we remained at the neighbor's house for the next several days. I knew once we returned home I would be in for the beating of my life.

My mother would be in a cast and crutches for the next two months.

"Young lady, I have not forgotten what you did. You set the backyard on fire and it could have spread to the house."

My father ordered me to my room. He would be in shortly to administer my punishment.

I didn't care. I had rescued my mother. Nothing else mattered. Out came the double wide, leather, black belt. He was clutching it in both hands, "Alright, pants down, turn over."

I buried my face into the blankets on top of the bed. With each lashing my father demanded to know, "why didn't I ever listen?" I buried my face as hard as I could, going deeper into the mattress each time the leather struck my bare back and bottom skin.

When my father finished beating me, I went to bed without supper and I was grounded for a week. I went into the bathroom to take a bath before I went to bed, but I couldn't get the material from my under pants unstuck from my skin. Instead I brushed my teeth and cried myself to sleep, whispering to God, asking, over and over, "Why?"

The next morning my ballerina-patterned sheets were blood stained. I cried believing I was going to get hit again for making a mess. So that I wouldn't get in trouble again, I took off the top sheet and hid it in the far end of my closet.

With only three weeks left of school before summer break, I planned my big escape. I would be running away from home as soon as school was over. I knew of a public campground I had attended with my Brownie troop the summer before. I planned to go there and live until I graduated. I had this crazy idea I could get a job and pay for a place to live and when I was settled in I would send for my mother. I felt responsible for my mother's safety. I was eleven years old, but believed our lives would magically fall into place if only I could get her away from my father. The vision of the police officer laughing it up with my father on the day of the fire proved to me no one cared about us. It was up to me to take charge.

When school ended for the summer I packed up what I needed inside of a sleeping bag. I had some coins and three, crisp one dollar bills in a crystal clear glass piggy bank. I could not get the paper money out so I smashed the glass bank into little pieces.

When it was dark, I told my mother I was going outside to put my bike in the backyard. She wouldn't know what I was doing because she was still recovering from her injuries. I carried the large sleeping bag out from the basement, and hid it in the bushes at the far end of the house.

The next morning I told my mother I had plans to go to a girlfriend's house to play for the day. My stomach felt sick for telling a lie. My mother was in bed, resting.

I kissed her on the cheek and told her, "I love you," and headed for the front door.

I didn't get very far, no more than a mile, when a station wagon with wooden side panels passed me, honking its horn. I picked up the pace and tried to walk faster, but the bag I was carrying was heavy. A voice called out to me.

"Susan? Susan! Come on, I'll give you a lift."

It was Pastor Dunne. He put my bag in the back seat.

He asked where I was going with such a heavy bag. I was not sure what to say. I blurted out, "I'm running away from home."

"Oh, were you going someplace far away?"

I mumbled the name of the campground.

"That's kind of far from here. Were you planning on walking all the way?"

"No sir. I was going to catch the #68 bus and then the number #15 to the train."

"I see. You have it all planned out. Does your mom know where you're going?"

"No. Why would I tell her? It's a secret. I'm running away."

"Did you leave her a note to say goodbye?"

"Nope, I didn't think about leaving a note."

"I have an idea and I bet you're hungry. Why don't we stop and get something to eat and I'll help you with the note and I'll give it to your mother so she doesn't worry about you."

"Okay," I said. "That's a good idea."

Pastor Dunne and I went to a nearby diner, sat down at a table and he pulled out a notepad and pen from his pocket and set them down. He leaned in from across the table.

"We can eat first, before we write the note."

As we ate, Pastor Dunne asked me, "Are you afraid of thunder storms? We're in for a big storm later tonight, with lots of lighting, thunder, and heavy rain."

I had a terrified look on my face and replied, " I'm afraid of lighting."

We finished our meal.

"What should we write?" he asked. "I know: 'Dear Mom, I don't want to make you sad, so I'm writing this note to tell you I ran away from home.' Does that sound okay with you?" the pastor asked.

"Do you want me to write down where you're going so your mom won't cry? She's going to be very sad when I give her this note."

I stared at the pastor, not knowing how to respond. "I don't want my mommy to be sad or cry." Tears streamed down my cheeks.

Ever so gently he asked, "Is your daddy hurting your mom?"

"Yes, but I'm not supposed to tell anybody, and anyway, nobody ever believes me," I replied.

"I believe you. Why don't you tell me? Maybe I can help."

"I can't. I'll get in trouble." I was sure of that.

"Susan, what you tell me will stay between the two of us. You won't get in trouble."

So I did. I told Pastor Dunne about setting the fire, and why I was running away.

"Nobody believes us. Even when the firemen and police came they didn't help us. I prayed to God, he didn't listen either. It's no use. I need to do this so we can be free."

Somehow Pastor Dunne talked me into going home. He would see what he could do so I would not be afraid. I begged him not to tell my mother.

Pastor Dunne gave me his word, his lips were sealed.

Pastor Dunne talked about a summer camp sponsored through the church, and he was going to discuss the details with my mother to see if I could go.

The camp was called Pine Trail Camp and was located in Michigan. I was excited about the possibility of being able to go away to camp.

In the car ride home Pastor Dunne told me to come to him when something was troubling me.

"Pastor, tell me how come I pray to God if he never listens to me?"

Pastor Dunne smiled. "Susan, God always listens and answers our prayers."

I interrupted. "No, he doesn't! I prayed for the longest time to make my dad stop hurting us and he didn't do anything. God never listens to me, ever!"

Pastor Dunne talked about how Jesus was God's son, "God sent him to this earth to die. He was nailed to a cross and he died for our sins. His name was Jesus."

I wanted to know what Jesus did that was so bad to be nailed on a cross?

"Nothing. God sent his son to this earth to wash away our sins"

"Huh? Now, I'm really confused," I said.

"How about I give you some storybooks and maybe you will understand when you read them? And, if you have questions, we can talk again," he told me.

I felt better after talking with Pastor Dunne, relieved I would not be alone in a big storm.

Funny thing, it never did rain that night.

Chapter Five
No Where to Run

Nine months to the day, after my father pulled us off the bus to make our escape for Ohio, my mother gave birth to a healthy baby girl.

They named her Patricia. Patricia's birth seemed like another way for my father to control my mother. With three children she was even less likely to attempt to leave anytime in the near future.

I met with Pastor Dunne to ask how God could bring another life into a family that lived in fear for their lives.

The Pastor said, "We have to trust God's timing and wisdom. The birth of each life is a blessing. God has his reasons. Enjoy your new baby sister. I will continue to pray for you and your family."

Politely, I thanked the pastor and returned home. But I left confused and scratching my head.

Later that evening, as I was preparing for bed, I prayed to God for an answer. "No offense, God," I said, "but Pastor Dunne wasn't much help. Maybe you could take a moment out of your busy day and help me understand. Thanks for listening. Amen."

My parents continued to have heated arguments.

After my mother gave birth to the baby, my father refused to sign legal documents allowing my mother's tubes to be tied. They argued about this in her hospital room. My mother accused my father of trying to teach her a lesson. With a smug look on my father's face he responded, "That's why they require 'permission' from the husband."

"There's nothing wrong or immoral about tying your tubes," she cried, "It's 1971, not 1921, you don't have the right to decide whether I have my tubes tied!"

"Roberta, the conversation is over. Stop your whining!"

My fifth grade teacher, Miss Lyons, gave our class a poetry assignments during Easter break. She instructed each of us to write a poem about something familiar. It could be about a pet, sports, the sunset, a family event.

I wrote my poem:

"Nowhere to Run"
My father drinks and carries a gun,
each night he comes home it's really no fun.
He beats my mom all bloody and blue,
Please, oh please, someone tell me what to do?
That bottle, that gun, we have no place to run.

The morning school bell rang and students situated themselves in their assigned seats. The teacher went row by row, and each student read his or her poem aloud to the class.

After everyone finished reading their assignments, the teacher instructed the class to study for a math test.

The teacher cleared her throat, "Susan Murphy, please come up to my desk. Bring your poem, dear."

In a low whisper she said to me, "Come with me."

As we left the classroom, she said out loud, "Class, I'll be right back. Continue studying."

We walked in silence down the long stretch of hallway, directly into the principal's office.

I was ordered to sit in the vacant chair outside the cloudy glass door marked in bold black letters "Principal's Office."

The teacher clutched my class assignment. She tapped on the door and entered.

"In trouble again," I mumbled to myself. Twenty minutes passed. Finally the teacher emerged, "Susan, go on in. The principal is waiting for you."

I thought to myself, "I didn't ask to see him."

I walked into the office with a silly grin on my face.

"Young lady, wipe that look off your face and sit down." A cigarette was burning in the ashtray. The principal was a tall, older man, with snow white hair, smoke stained teeth, and square black framed glasses. The principal was holding my poem.

He read it out loud.

When he was finished he threw it across the desk towards me. "What's this garbage? Why would you write this?"

I shrugged my shoulders.

The principal raised his voice, "That's not an answer!"

I mumbled, "It's true. I'm not lying to you."

"Lies, young lady, lies! I'm disgusted with you! You will rewrite this assignment and turn it into me."

I responded, "No, I will not."

"That's it! I've had it with you!"

Again, for the second time, my school file was in front of another school principal.

As the principal dialed my home number, he said to me, "You're an angry, rotten child, seeking attention and drama. I will not tolerate your insubordination."

"Hello, Mrs. Murphy, this is Principal Burke. Um, Yes, I'm well, thank you. I'm calling to ask if you and Mr. Murphy are available sometime tomorrow for a conference in my office regarding Susan. Great, I'll see you at 10:30 tomorrow morning."

He hung up the phone.

The principal stretched his neck across the desk. "Go back to class. Return to my office tomorrow at 10:30 AM"

I went to my school locker, thinking no one would miss me.

"I'm not going back to class," I said to myself.

Knowing my father was out of town on a hunting trip, I went straight home.

Every year my father went with his fellow police officers to hunt in Michigan and fish in Canada. We had the best time when my father was on his "trips." My mother would plan special meals.

We all slept better when we knew he was not coming home. Sometimes my mother would turn on the stereo or radio while we played card games like Fish and Old Maid. It was just so much better when he wasn't around.

My foot didn't even get in the door before my mother asked me the question, "What'd you do now?"

I explained what happened. My mother said it would be okay. She gave me a big hug, we played with the baby, and watched television together.

The following day, my mother arrived at school with Patricia sound asleep in the baby stroller.

When I got to the principal's office at 10:30, my mom was already seated across from his desk.

The principal spoke as if I had stolen the milk money from the lunchroom. He offered suggestions from counseling to suspension. He went so far as to imply I may have a mental retardation situation that was never properly diagnosed. My mother assured him she would handle the matter.

"You're released from class for the remainder of the day."

"Yes, sir." I hung my head down low until the two of us were out of sight, away from the school.

On the walk home, my mom suggested that we stop and have lunch. My mother was not good with words. Mostly she cried when she was uncomfortable and didn't know what to say.

Delicately, she explained the circumstances under which we had to live. She apologized for the principal's behavior. "I'm so proud of you, and you wrote a wonderful poem. What happened at school today is our 'little secret.'"

Mom reached over and held my hand.

"I love you, and I'm very proud of you. How about we order ice-cream sodas for dessert?"

At age twelve I was given permission to take jobs babysitting for families in the neighborhood. Every penny I earned from babysitting went into the bank. I had high hopes of being rich. That someday I was going to take my mother and my baby sister far, far away.

The same year, I entered womanhood, and my mother sat me down and we had "the talk." Awkwardly, she explained how babies are born. "No one should ever do anything to you, you know, down in your female private parts." I giggled as my mother tried to explain the birds and the bees.

My pre-teen years were awkward. My feet had grown to a size nine and I noticed my breasts were larger than those of other classmates. I was clumsy, always tripping over my own two feet and I was also taller and heavier than all the girls in class. I didn't fit in and looked as if I were in high school.

One day, the 7th grade math teacher pulled me and two other girls out of class and into the hall for a talk. She handed each girl a pamphlet from Weight Watchers, "I noticed you three could use some guidance on nutrition."

We were in shock. We didn't know how to respond.

The teacher was informing us that we were fat.

When I brought the pamphlet home I threw it in the garbage.

That night, I refused dinner. My mother thought I was getting sick, and went to take my temperature.

"No, Mom, I'm fine."

"But you didn't have supper. What's the matter?"

"Nothing." I paused. Then said, "The teacher handed me and two other girls a Weight Watchers booklet and said we needed to go on a diet."

My brother immediately began taunting me, "Susie is a fatso, Susie is a," in mid-sentence my mother interrupted, "Stop that right now. Go do something with yourself in the other room."

"Honey, you don't need to go on a diet. You're at that stage most young girls experience, in between a teenager and an adult. You'll slim down when nature says it's time, and not before. The teacher should not have put that into your head. I'm going to go to the school and have a talk with her."

I didn't want to be embarrassed. All I needed was for my mother, who was overweight herself, to go and visit the teacher.

"No please, I'll eat. Can we forget about this, please?" I said.

She hesitated for a moment before agreeing not to speak with the teacher.

When school ended for summer break, my mother allowed me to attend Pine Trail Camp for two weeks. In church, Pastor Dunne talked about the experience of kids from other churches around the country attending camp.

The church would arrange for a bus. It was a three-hour trip each way.

In preparation for camp Pastor Dunne explained, "You're representing our church, so I expect you all to behave like ladies and gentlemen and there's one more requirement, as you board the bus for camp, you're expected to recite a verse from the Holy Bible."

I didn't know any verses, and I was not really very good at memorizing anything. I tore apart my bedroom closet looking for the Bible I was given at Sunday school the year before.

Finally, after about an hour of rummaging around the bottom of my closet, I found the Bible. I decided the easiest way to select a Bible verse was to shut my eyes, open the book and point to a verse. I wrote out the verse by hand in a school notebook, and on several other pieces of paper I copied the verse, taping it to various locations in my bedroom.

I was so excited to be going away. But I was concerned about leaving my mother alone for such a long period of time.

Two days before camp, I pretended to be sick. My mother sensed my fear.

"Honey, I'm fine. Your father will be on his fishing trip to Canada and he returns the day after you return from camp. I want you to go and have a good time. No more silly talk. How about we find you a duffel bag and start preparing for your trip?"

Close to fifty kids waited outside the church lawn with their suitcases and duffel bags along the sidewalk.

Pastor Dunne arrived with the bus. One by one, each kid got on, reciting a verse before taking a seat.

I waited patiently, then, when it was my turn proudly recited my passage: "For God so loved the world that he gave his only begotten Son; that whosoever believeth in him shall not perish but have everlasting life. John 3:16."

"Nice job, Susan. You recited the most important verse in the Bible!"

I didn't know the importance of that particular verse.

As I walked to an empty seat, I glowed with pride for remembering the verse and because of Pastor Dunne's comments to me.

The experience at summer camp would have a profound effect on me.

Owned by a Baptist pastor and his wife, Pine Trail Camp brought kids together from all around the Midwest to learn the word of God while having fellowship and creating spiritual growth.

When we arrived the bus driver unloaded the luggage. We were assigned rustic wooden cabins with double rows of bunk beds.

Each morning campers awoke to the sounds of some off-beat, corny music playing over the camp's loud speaker. Before breakfast, each cabin competed against one another for prizes—the cleanest cabin, the best decorated or best themed. Cabins also won for staging practical gags when the camp counselors inspected the cabins. It was fun.

Meals were eaten in a large, clean mess hall. Campers were expected to bring their Bibles to breakfast, and after dinner everyone was required to be in the main hall for prayer break-out sessions, where we would talk about God and ask questions.

During one lunch a tall, freckled, red-haired girl sat beside me, "Hi, my name is Kathryn. What's your name?"

"Susan," I replied as I checked the time on the mess hall clock.

"Hey, can I ask, where do you go every day?"

"No place special," I answered before excusing myself from the table.

I always snuck off to wade in the river.

I had never known such peace. One evening a camp counselor caught me leaving out the back door of the main hall building during the evening Bible study.

"Where do you think you're going?" asked the counselor.

"To the river," I replied.

"What's so important on the river?"

"There's no place like this back home. It's where I go to figure things out, listen to the fish jump about in the water. Or the frogs croaking," I said.

The camp counselor smiled at me. "Alright, go ahead, but don't stay out there all night."

I think the only reason I was given permission was because the counselor knew it was important to me. About an hour later, I heard a voice call my name. "Hey, I was looking all over for you."

It was Kathryn, she said, "I brought my Bible and thought we could read together for while."

Kathryn was from North Carolina. Her grandparents were missionaries, her father was a deacon at a church and she had six brothers and sisters. I knew all about her in twenty seconds.

When Kathryn suggested we head back for prayer and bed, I told her I was staying.

"You know this is against camp rules?" she said to me.

"Kathryn, my counselor knows where I am. You go on ahead and I'll see you at breakfast."

The following night I wasn't so lucky. An announcement was made at breakfast that campers were expected to participate in all activities, unless they had a medical excuse from the nurse which meant no more sneaking out for me.

I decided to wait until everyone was asleep in the cabin, pull my sleeping bag from the bunk and make my way down to the river. Sometimes I would go when the sun was rising. It was so beautiful. Never before had I felt so calm and peaceful.

At camp we were expected to write letters or postcards home. I didn't write much more than I missed everyone and would be home soon.

Along with Bible study and fellowship, the camp provided group related activities and for the first time I felt comfortable in my own skin. I was not judged. I made friends with other kids my own age. The two weeks went by quickly. The final night of camp, as I lay peacefully in my sleeping bag counting the stars in the sky, Kathryn walked up the hill, "mind if I join you?" she asked. The two of us laughed and talked under the bright stars all night in our sleeping bags.

As I was preparing to head home, Kathryn ran over to say good-bye to me. We exchanged addresses promising to write until next year when we returned to camp.

Pastor Dunne was waiting in the church parking lot to welcome us home.

Everyone got off the bus, the only kid who didn't have a parent meet and greet them was me. Picking up the large duffel bag, I started to walk home. Pastor Dunne offered to give me a lift.

"You look splendid, Susan. Did you have a good time?"

With a smile on my face, I replied, "Yes! It was lots of fun. I want to go back next year."

I rarely smiled and it seemed to warm the pastor's heart to witness me glowing from the inside out with joy.

My mother was happy to have me home. We had a day of peace and quiet before my father returned from his fishing trip. My mother, brother, sister, and I enjoyed a pleasant evening together.

These times together would be rare, similar to celebrating a birthday once a year.

The time at camp changed me. I found myself reciting John 3:16 at different times throughout my day. When my father would come home and battle with my mother, I would run the verse through my head. It gave me hope.

It was around this time I met with Pastor Dunne. I wanted to be baptized, to experience more of the journey of God's love. Although I really didn't understand what I was suppose to know about God, I knew for sure going to hell was not an option.

The Catholic Church held no importance to me other than I was baptized as a baby so my father could publicly claim his kids were Catholic. My father was a strong Irish Catholic in name only. He never went to church unless it was to attend the funeral service of a relative or fellow officer.

Chapter Six
Mutilation of a Child's Spirit

I wanted to know what a person had to do in order to get to heaven when they died.

At camp I learned you first had to accept Jesus Christ as your Lord and Savior. In picking the most important verse in the Bible as my memory verse, I took that as a sign from God.

After school, I stopped by the church and talked to Pastor Dunne. "I'm ready to accept Jesus Christ as my personal savior. I want to be baptized in the church," I announced.

Pastor Dunne replied, "Susan, you were baptized as a baby. It's not required of you. You can accept Christ without being baptized."

"No, Pastor Dunne, you have to baptize me. I don't want to end up in hell. Please, Pastor Dunne." I don't think Pastor Dunne thought he could convince my mother and that is why he tried to talk me out of being baptized.

"Susan, I can assure you, you won't go hell." Pastor Dunne studied my face, then he added, "Alright, I'll baptize you in the church."

The Pastor met with my mother to discuss the details of my baptism. My mother was perplexed. As children, each of us was baptized in the Catholic church six weeks after we were born. She didn't understand the significance of doing it again. Pastor Dunne, knowing my mother was raised Jewish, explained it in terms that related to her religion. "Consider this a Baptist bat mitzvah, if you will. Susan feels this is important for her to accept God at this time in her life. And this is common for those who have accepted Jesus Christ as their Lord and Savior to want the baptismal service."

"But how will we do this?" my mother asked. "You print announcements in the paper don't you? I can't take the chance of her father finding out. He would be furious. My husband only believes in the Catholic Church."

"Mrs. Murphy, sensing this could cause a problem, I have cleared this unique situation with the deacons at the church. They have granted me permission to perform a private ceremony on a day and time convenient to you, and it will not be announced in a church bulletin or the newspaper. I will require two witnesses to be present at the baptism. One will be my wife and I was hoping the other would be you."

"Alright," my mom said, "but if I'm unable to participate, do you have someone else who would be able to be there?"

"Why certainly," he replied. "but please try to attend. This really is important to your daughter."

My mother continued to make dates with Pastor Dunne for me to be baptized, only to cancel them a day or two before.

My mother didn't feel comfortable leaving the house with black and blue bruises all over her arms and legs.

Six months later I was finally baptized. At the last minute my mother was too embarrassed to come. She didn't have anything nice to wear and had too many bruises. All the same, I had an amazing experience.

Pastor Dunne asked me if I was ready to accept Jesus Christ as my Lord and Savior. Placing a white handkerchief over my face Pastor Dunne gently held me, bending me backwards and dunking me in the small baptismal pool behind the church pulpit.

The Pastor's wife and a handful of other church members and I went downstairs where we had a small party in celebration of my new journey. I don't know that I felt any different. Though, I wanted to feel renewed, changed somehow, but when you don't have any idea how to experience joy you act as I did, without any emotion.

School continued to bore me. I attended because I didn't have a choice. The only goal in my immediate future was to get my mother away from my father, alive.

The following summer, I returned to Pine Trial Camp. Again, we were required to recite a bible verse. This would be easy. I used the same verse the from last year, but this time, I said it faster. I didn't pull the wool over Pastor Dunne's eyes.

He raised his brow and chuckled, "Susan, if you're going to repeat the same verse as last year, at least say the verse slowly and with meaning."

When I returned from camp my mother announced she was going to have surgery. She had always complained of female problems but frankly I always attributed her complaints to the abuse.

The doctor told my mother she required surgery. He scheduled a hysterectomy. After surgery, she would remain in the hospital for ten days. I was to come home straight from school and watch my little sister.

The night after her surgery, my father returned home, roaring drunk. My brother was asleep downstairs and Patricia was at the other end of the house, asleep.

While I was asleep, my father walked into my room. Startled, I awoke sensing danger. Trapped in the corner of my bed, with my father blocking the doorway. The foul putrid smell of stale alcohol and tobacco filled the air.

I didn't know what to do or say. I knew this was not a dream.

My father came into the room. I began to tremble, "Get out, get the hell out of my room now." I demanded.

In a drunken slur, I only heard, "Shut up." He set down his glass of vodka and ice on my dresser.

"Oh my God, what are you doing?" I said, trying to stand up and get away. With the front side of his hand I was slapped up against the wall and went further into the corner of the bed. The next thing I remember he was on top of me like dead weight. I couldn't breathe or move.

I tried to kick, bite, pinch, anything to get him off of me. He slapped me across the face again. Then he covered my mouth with his hand.

"Be quiet, do you hear me." My head was shaking back and forth in protest. His entire hand remained firm around my mouth and chin. I was soaked through the bed sheets in my own sweat, trembling with fear. At that very moment all I kept thinking about is wanting to die. Repeatedly, over and over in my head, I asked God why? I wanted to die.

"Don't be scared. This isn't going to hurt you," he muttered.

He lifted up my pajama top. I fought him. I was finally able to get my mouth open enough to bite his wrist as hard as I could.

"Son of a bitch," he screamed. He raised his hand up high into the air and knocked me out cold.

When I came too, I had difficulty focusing my raw, swollen eyes in my bedroom. Shelves once anchored securely on the walls displaying stuffed animals and glass figurines were now on the floor. The smell of alcohol mixed with cheap after shave remained on me, the bedding, and in the air. I was freezing cold, my pajama's were on the floor, by the bed. I was bloody. On my dresser were my father's service revolver, his wallet, handcuffs, and his empty vodka glass.

I heard Patricia crying for someone to come and get her. I wasn't sure what to do. My little sister's screams grew louder. "Coming, Patty," I shouted.

I heard Bobby coming up from his bedroom in the basement. Rising from my bed I pulled open a drawer, and grabbed a shirt from the dresser. With every ounce of strength I pulled it over my head, down around my body.

I called to Bobby, "please open Patty's door and give her some cereal. I'll be there in a few minutes." I swung my door shut. I stared at the service revolver on the dresser. The thought crossed my mind to end all the insanity now, I didn't want to live. But I kept hearing a voice in my head saying, "you must stay strong and brave for your mother." And I could not bring myself to touch the gun. I was afraid if I picked it up the wrong way it would discharge by itself. What was I going to do?

I rocked in a fetal position for what seemed like an eternity. I was finally startled by Patty. She had finished her cereal and wanted to come in my room. I covered the top of the dresser with a blanket. I diverted my sister's attention enough that I could sneak into the bathroom and get cleaned up. I held myself up over the sink, staring blankly in the mirror.

Completely unable to make sense of what just happened. Trying to gather my thoughts as to where I could go for help. I needed to tell someone. But after not being believed and labeled as the child who just told stories, I felt completely helpless. At that moment an anger I never thought possible consumed me. I was helpless. I didn't like being held hostage by a man who society honored just because he happened to be cop. I hated my father for what he did to me and vowed that someday, when I was old enough, I would get us all away from him.

Suddenly, an overwhelming surge came over me and I threw up in the sink. My face was badly bruised and swollen. I mustered every ounce of strength and went into shower. My knees dropped down to the porcelain tub and I cried as the scalding hot water hit my neck and back. I remained there until the water became cold. I went back into my room trying to decide if I could call anyone for help?

Patty was making a fuss. I called out to Bobby, went into my father's wallet and slipped a twenty dollar bill under the door. Bribing Bobby into dressing Patty and taking her to the dime store and buying her a toy.

I removed the soiled sheets from my bed and replaced them with cleans ones. I couldn't stop trembling and wrapped myself up in a heavy blanket before climbing back into the bed. A few minutes later, my father entered my room.

"I wouldn't talk about this to anyone if I were you. No one will believe you. And if I find out you did tell your mother or a teacher at school, I'll have you locked up and committed someplace far away." As he gathered his personal items and gun from the dresser top, he asked, "am I making myself clear?"

All I could do was stare past him as he spoke.

Before leaving the room he walked up to the bed to look at my face. As he began to extend his hand, I shot my body back up against the wall in fear.

I continued to lay there and think about what to do next. I dressed and began packing a bag. My head was in a fog. Still not sure what I was going to do. I was not staying one more night alone in this house while my mother was in the hospital. I decided to go down the street to Jackie's, our neighbor, for help.

Jackie was my sister's Godmother. She agreed to take Patty for the next ten days.

When she asked me about my face, I didn't answer because I didn't believe if I told her she could help me. Since my grandparents were on vacation, I used the spare key we kept in the house and stayed at their apartment. I thought Bobby would be alright by himself as long as he could have dinner down the street with Jackie.

"Jackie, One more favor to ask, could you come back with me to the house while I get some stuff and then drop me off at the bus depot."

I'm sure she knew something was terribly wrong, because I choked up and couldn't speak.

"Susie, I'll do whatever you need me to do." she replied.

We walked back to the house. My father opened the door. I slipped past him while he and Jackie spoke. I grabbed a bag, went out the back door and walked to the front. She told my father the girls were staying with her and it would better because of his schedule. She would make sure we were fed and watched. Later that night I arrived at my grandparent's apartment.

I was never the same. I was robbed by my father. He was a thief, just like someone who held up a store for money.

My father took much more from me than I could ever imagine. He hijacked my spirit and my soul all at the same time.

I didn't visit my mother while she remained in the hospital, making excuses that I had homework to finish until the bruising faded. I was determined, more than ever after the brutal attack by my father, to leave. But I couldn't. I felt strongly if I did leave that my mother would die. I took responsibility for her life.

When she returned home from the hospital she kept asking me to confide in her. My mother could sense something was terribly wrong. Somehow I convinced her I was fine. What other choice did I have? I believed my father when he said he would have me locked up and sent away.

I barely passed the 8th grade. Preparing for graduation was an event I would rather forget. The only store carrying plus size clothes for girls like me was Lane Byrant. For the occasion, my mother insisted we go shopping for a formal dress at the "oversized" store. I was so embarrassed.

My mother bought me the only dress in the store that fit. A polyester one that had green trim and cherries with leaves covering the dress. The pattern looked as though it came from a tablecloth.

It was not flattering on me. I was not given a choice. All the girls in my class had pretty dresses. To try and make me feel better, my mother told me it was because I was taller and they were shorter and petite.

I said, "what you mean to say is that they're thin and pretty. I'm large and fat."

I spent most of the summer earning money babysitting for kids in the neighborhood. I found excuses not to be home if I knew my father was anywhere around.

The same year, 1974, President Nixon resigned as President of the United States, I was entering high school, and I was not looking forward to it at all.

Nearly five feet nine inches tall and two hundred and thirty eight pounds, my baby fat was still hanging onto my hips.

My attire during freshman year consisted of blue jeans and button down flannel shirts to cover my baby fat. I avoided the freshman ritual better known as initiation. I didn't look or act the part of a freshman. The upper classmen ignored me.

My high school offered a program to become a licensed practical nurse, which piqued my interest. When I discovered how little it paid though I quickly decided to take a pass.

As a freshman, I looked more like a 19-year-old. My appearance allowed me to work evenings and night hours. Having a job was my way to shake off the extra layer of fear now sticking to me, courtesy of my father, like permanent glue. Being away and out of the house each day gave me the chance to breathe without constantly being in fear of the unknown.

On weekends, I worked at the neighborhood drugstore behind the counter. One of the perks included all the candy I could eat at work. During the week I was a nurse's assistant at a local nursing home, although I was really nothing more than a glorified bed pan collector. I loved the residents and the hourly wage they paid me. I saved almost everything I earned. I still had a plan to leave the day I turned eighteen and I would be taking my mother with me.

I barely passed my subjects in school though. At least once a week I was in the school counselor's office for mouthing off to a teacher because I didn't do my homework, or had skipped class. I was unable to focus. School wasn't going to pave the road for my mother's freedom. Earning enough money, so I could get her away from my father, was my priority.

I continued attending church and making new friends. I didn't drink or get into trouble.

During my sophomore year I decided I would work on my appearance. I wanted to be accepted by my classmates. I knew I would have to change my poor eating habits and dress more like a lady to do this.

I was still working at the nursing home. The Thanksgiving holiday was a few days away, but I had no intention of being home. I was going to work a double-shift.

My father overheard me talking to my mother. I was not planning on being home for Thanksgiving dinner.

"What's this I hear? Where do you think you're going?" he questioned.

"I'm working a double shift for double the hourly pay," I said.

"No you're not! You'll be home for Thanksgiving with your family," said my father, sternly.

My mother tried to defend me but the moment my father put his foot forward, as though he was going to lunge at her, she backed off, watching, and standing helplessly.

"I don't think so. I don't want to be here. I'm going to work," I declared.

He whacked me so hard across the face with the back of his hand that I fell down the back steps of the landing at the backdoor.

I grabbed my coat and went to a girlfriend's house for a couple hours.

Thanksgiving morning, around 4:30 AM, my father came into my bedroom and ordered me to get ready. I was going someplace with him.

We argued. I had to be at work in a couple of hours.

"No you don't. I called you in sick. Now get up, wash your face, brush your teeth, and put some clothes on. You're coming with me!"

I was afraid to go with him alone. I thought he was going to take me someplace and hurt me. Or, because I'd disobeyed him, he was going to drive me far away and lock me up. When I asked where we were going he ordered me to shut up and get in the car.

I was alone with my father for the first time since the assault. My father and I didn't speak in the car. I sat as close to the passenger door as possible, my hand on the door lever preparing to jump out just in case he tried to hurt me or drive far enough out of the way that I couldn't run for help. I didn't ask where it was he was taking me. I repeatedly told myself, "don't give him the satisfaction of smelling your fear."

He pulled up to a dimly lit church parking lot. We were warmly greeted by an elderly Catholic priest who was directing food and supplies inside.

The priest extended his hand to my father, "Phillip, what an unexpected surprise." By the conversation they obviously had known one another for years.

"Hi Father. This is my daughter, Susan. She'll be helping you out for the day. I'll pick her up around 6:00 this evening."

He handed the priest his card with our home telephone number on the back.

"If she gives you any trouble, call me and I'll come and get her."

In a thick Irish brogue, "Phillip, my son, I'm sure we'll have no trouble."

My father shot me his famous "or else" look as he headed for the door.

I was going into a mission facility for the poor where they expected to feed close to 2,000 families Thanksgiving dinner. I was kept in the kitchen the better part of the morning. At the noon hour the doors to the large dining hall opened. The person in charge of the volunteer's in the kitchen had me go to a hot table and serve mashed potatoes and gravy to homeless families. Everyone was very orderly and waited patiently to be served a hot holiday meal of turkey and all the trimmings.

A lot of those I served looked as though they had not had a bath in a long time. Their faces were filthy and several men had knotted beards and long, dirty, finger nails. I noticed most of the men were in need of dental care. Very few had teeth.

Mothers with children came up to me asking if they could wait around and take home any leftovers. It was very disturbing to see all these people under one roof with no place to call home.

We were so busy serving food, the time went by quickly. My father was in the kitchen waiting for me at six on the dot to take me back home.

The Irish priest tapped me on the shoulder, thanking me for my service.

Of course, my father inquired as to my attitude, before we headed for home.

The priest told my father, "She was the best worker we had all day. Thank you for bringing your daughter to help."

On the ride back my father asked me if I learned anything.

I had to be careful how to respond or I would end up out in the middle of nowhere on some dark, isolated road.

"Yes, it was interesting," I said.

My father gave me a lecture on those less fortunate, who make their homes on the streets. He wanted me to understand how lucky I was to have family who loved me and a roof over my head.

I bit the side of my cheek so I would stop myself from talking back to my father.

When we returned home, my mother had dinner ready.

"I'm not hungry. I'm going to bed."

"Susan, go wash your hands. You're sitting at the dinner table and having Thanksgiving dinner with your family," my father said.

"I'm sorry, I'm going to bed," I replied.

My father dragged me in the bathroom and began beating me for disobeying his command. I realized that no matter what he did to me, I no longer cared.

"Go ahead, slap me some more," I said. "Take off your belt and beat me like you do Mom. You're nothing but a coward who beats up women! Come on, I dare you! Hit me some more!"

I do not know where the courage came from to speak to my father in that way. Suddenly, my father stopped hitting me. He walked out of the bathroom and into the living room.

I could hear the top of the vodka bottle open and the sound of the alcohol as it met the crackling ice cubes in the glass.

My mother tended to my bloody nose.

I whispered to her, "I'm leaving. I'll be back later."

"Stay here and go to bed. Don't go," my mother pleaded.

I shook my head no. I was leaving the house.

I went into my bedroom and packed my uniform for work in the morning.

I kissed my mother on the cheek and slipped out the back door. I stayed over at a girlfriend's house for the night.

The next day, I worked a double shift at the nursing home.

When I came home, my mother and sister were curled up on the living room couch, asleep with the television on. My mother heard me come in and smiled warmly. When she smiled it made me smile.

"Are you okay, honey?" my mother asked.

"Yes, I'm fine."

"Could you carry your sister into bed?"

"Yeah, sure."

"How about I fix you something to eat?"

"No, mom. I ate earlier. I'm not hungry."

I made myself scarce for the next several days. I didn't want to have another run-in with my father.

Things stayed quiet around the house for a few weeks, but it didn't last long. My father went on one of his drinking binges and was missing in action for a few days.

I was awakened to the sound of my father yelling at my mother, demanding that she, "get her lazy, fat ass out of bed," and fix him something to eat. When my mother asked him where he had been for three days, he responded by telling her to, "Shut up, I'm hungry."

My father then grabbed my mother by her hair and threw her head into the burners on top of the stove. The blow opened a large, deep gash above her eye.

I had just gotten my driver's permit and since my father was too drunk to drive my mother to the hospital, I grabbed a towel and had my mother put pressure on the injury. I located my father's car keys.

My father was eating straight from the refrigerator, his eyes barely open. He was holding himself up by the refrigerator door, swaying back and forth. It was a disgusting sight. My mother bled through the towel.

I had to get her to the hospital. I went to my sister's bedroom and got her dressed.

I went outside. The car was not there. I came back into the house. "Mom, someone must've given Dad a ride home. His car isn't here. I'm going to call a cab." I shook my head, signaling that my mother not ask my father any questions.

Within ten minutes, the taxi arrived.

I carried my little sister, who was still sleeping, in my arms. The three of us went to the hospital.

At the hospital, they stitched my mother up and we headed back to the house.

My father, still in his clothes, was passed out in the bedroom.

He had solved a major case and, as a reward, his boss gave him a few days off.

My brother's bedroom was downstairs in the basement. He slept through all the commotion.

When my father woke up, he took a handful of aspirin, called into the office, asking if someone at the station could pick him up for work. It seems my father was too drunk after his shift to drive home.

A fellow officer had taken his car keys away and the car was left in the police parking lot overnight.

An hour or so later, he was out the door.

"Mom, how much more of this are you going to take?" I asked.

My mother started crying.

"Leave her alone, it's not her fault. Dad's a jerk," my brother said.

Susan (5) with her brother Bobby (4). A Sears portrait that was a fixture on the console tv from the day mother received it.

Susan, age 2

This is the only photo my parents ever took together.

Susan, holding her doll, Molly

Chapter Seven
Prisoner of Fear

My father was gentle when it came to my sister Patricia. They had a connection as father and daughter. I cannot recall him ever raising his voice or hand to her in anger. Patricia was my father's precious little girl.

Patricia was his baby, but I still feared my father would sexually abuse her. I tried to shield Patricia from everything. If she was sleeping and my father's rages sent my mother into the hospital, I made up excuses for Patricia that mom got sick in the middle of the night and had to go to the hospital. Patricia didn't have the same fear my brother and I experienced when we were her age.

One day my mother declared, "I was thinking of taking driving lessons. We won't be able to tell your father, of course. I thought after I learned to drive, and after Patricia starts school, I'd go and look for a job." A few months later, my mother enrolled in driving school. I would watch my sister on the nights she was taking her lessons.

One night, my father came home unexpectedly at the dinner hour. "Where's your mother?" he asked.

"She went out for a few minutes," I replied. "She'll be right back"

"Where the hell did your mother go? Why isn't she home?"

I replied I didn't know where she went.

A half hour later, Mom walked in the front door. She didn't know my father was home. His unmarked squad car was parked at the end of the block.

The moment my mother walked through the front door she started chirping like a canary.

"Chuck says I'll be ready to take the driving test next week."

My father walked in from the kitchen. He had a crazy look in his eyes.

"Who the hell is Chuck? And where have you been?"

It was the first time I witnessed my mother stand up to my father.

"I'm taking driving lessons. Chuck is my driving instructor. I'm going to learn how to drive, and then I'm going to get a job."

"Oh, is that right, Roberta? Where are you taking driving lessons?"

"The Central-A-One Driving School over off Foster Avenue."

Infuriated, my father stormed out of the house.

The following day, the teacher at the driving school called the house, informing my mother she was not able to return for lessons. He was refunding half of her money. I found out my father went and paid the man a visit. He threatened to have the driving school shut down for some violation if he gave my mother another driving lesson. My mother didn't back down. A few weeks later, she figured out a way to resume her lessons at another driving school.

At thirty-five years of age, my mother received her driver's license, and, of course, didn't tell my father, keeping it a secret for several months. Once my sister started grade school, my mother bought a second hand car with money she had managed to save. A week later my mother applied for a job as a customer service representative with a large Fortune 500 company. My mother broke the news to my father.

As one would imagine, my father didn't receive the news well at all, and ordered my mother to contact the company and decline the job. My mother refused. She no longer cared what he thought. My mother was going to work while my sister was at school. My father chased after my mother as she left the room.

Patricia screamed, "Daddy, Daddy, what are you doing?"

"Oh, sweetheart," my father replied as he came back into the room. "Mommy and Daddy are playing a game, that's all. Come here and give Daddy a kiss. I have to go back to work."

I wanted to puke at my father's phony insincere display of fatherly affection.

My mother started her job, and it was rough for several weeks. My father was doing things to get her to quit. He would wake her up from a sound sleep when he came home, or would take away her car keys.

But each morning, when my mother took my sister to school, she went to work.

On my eighteenth birthday I moved out of my parents' house and took an apartment a few miles away. I was interested in business. I learned of an intern position with a brokerage firm in downtown Chicago. I interviewed and was hired on the spot.

Around the same time, I shed my baby fat and blossomed into a swan. There were not enough hours in the day. On weekends I worked as a cocktail waitress in an upscale disco dance club. The money was fantastic. Working in a club taught me how to handle myself around men. Until then, I was awkward and unsure of myself. I hadn't really dated. The job at the club was a great life experience for me. I didn't drink, although everyone else around me did.

One night after work, I was closing up the bar and a young woman was passed out at the other end of the bar. The manager turned on all the lights, and approached the woman, informing her it was time to go. We were closed. She was too drunk to drive. The manager called her a cab.

The woman was stinking drunk. She looked familiar to me. I recognized her from school. She was only a couple years older than me. The woman looked older because she was a heavy drinker. Her makeup was smeared. She slurred her words. "Disgusting," I said to myself. "That will never be me." From that day forward I vowed never to get drunk. A drunken woman was an ugly woman.

My mother called me out of the blue one day to inform me she had met with a lawyer.

"I'm divorcing your father. Bobby is getting ready to leave for college and I'm taking Patricia to Florida. While we're gone, a sheriff will serve your father with divorce papers. I signed everything today. I paid the retainer to the lawyer. Temporarily, Patricia and I will move in with you. After the divorce is final, I'll buy a condo."

I looked up at the ceiling and said, "Thank you, God!"

I was very proud of my mother. I drove my sister and mother to the airport.

While they were in Florida, I needed some documents that were at my parents' house. Without thinking, I put my key in the front door and walked in. It never crossed my mind to ask my mother when my father was going to be served with the divorce papers.

Upon opening the front door to the house, I was met with a gun pointed in my direction. My heart did a triple summersault.

"What are you doing here?" My father growled.

I was so shaken by the gun I just about pissed in my pants. "I came for some documents in my room. I need to go to the bathroom. Excuse me," I said, as I walked slowly past him.

I noticed several guns on the kitchen table. Apparently, he was cleaning his gun collection.

Momentarily safe in the bathroom, I thought, "There is only one way out of this bathroom. I cannot escape." I had to think. I placed my head between my knees and took several deep breaths to calm down. I prayed to God to get me out safely.

When I finished in the bathroom, my father was sitting at the kitchen table cleaning his guns.

I went into my old bedroom and located the documents.

"Okay, I'm going." I called to him.

"No! Wait!" he yelled, "I want to talk to you."

"I have to get back to work." I replied.

My father was holding a gun in his hand as he was talking to me. I didn't know if it was loaded.

"Come here, please. I want you to read something." He handed me the 9 x 12 official envelope. "Susan, read it out loud."

I read it. Then my father asked if I knew anything about it.

"I had no idea," I said,

"Twenty years, I have been married to your mother and you know I never so much as cashed one lousy paycheck. I always handed them over to her. And this is how she repays me. A sheriff came to the house today and served me like a criminal. Do you have any idea how embarrassing that was? Huh, do you know?"

"Dad, I swear, I don't know anything. I didn't know she was going to do this."

Sweat was pouring from every pore in my body. All I wanted to do was run out of that house as fast as my legs would take me.

"I love your mother and you kids. You're my world." It was the first time I ever saw my father break down and cry. A large revolver was sitting in his lap. He went on babbling, for what seemed like eternity.

Slowly, I walked backwards from the kitchen into the living room and out the front door, all the time with my eyes on my father,

"I really have to go," I said.

He got up from the kitchen chair, a gun still in his hand, and walked towards me.

Once I had my hand on the doorknob, I said goodbye again and left.

I drove as fast as humanly possible back to my apartment.

I called my mother at the hotel, but there was no answer.

I left a message at the hotel desk to have her call me immediately. It was an emergency.

Later that evening, I finally reached my mother. I was upset. Being in the house with my father could have gone either way. He could have harmed me or kept me there against my will. My voice cracked as I relayed what happened.

A few days after my father was served with the papers, he got on a flight to Florida. A week later, my mother, sister, and father returned home.

I didn't have a good feeling about this. My mother called and invited me to dinner at the house. I refused. "Please," she begged, suggesting, in a pleading tone, we meet at nearby restaurant together and talk. It was an odd phone call. Reluctantly, the following weekend, I met them for dinner.

It was not a comfortable dinner. You know how, in the movies, when you see someone is being held at gunpoint trying to talk you away from a house and out of danger? That is how the entire evening felt. It was tense and rehearsed, staged to make me believe everything was alright.

My father kept a more watchful eye on my mother and her activities after they returned from Florida. I later learned my mother had dropped the divorce action. When my father went to Florida he was sweet as sugar. Once he got her away from my kid sister and they talked privately, he informed my mother that her children would be orphans if she went through with the divorce.

She was given a choice, which was really no choice: remain like a prisoner of war with my father, or be killed.

"When the time's right, I'll go." my mother told me.

I was furious with the situation. Her plan was to wait until my little sister was out of school before attempting to leave my father.

I tried to get her to move into the apartment with me. I believed it was far too dangerous for her to stay with him.

A few years passed and I was working at a large investment banking firm. I was close to moving my mother out of the house. My worst fear continued to be that one day she would be gone, that my father would make good on his chilling promise: "If you ever leave, I will find you. If I find you, Roberta, I will kill you."

My brother Bobby was in college attending a university downstate. He wanted to be a lawyer. After I moved out of the house, we seldom spoke. Once in while he would call me at work, asking me to send him money. Out of left field my brother dropped out of school. It made no sense. Bobby was on the Dean's List.

When he didn't come home or call, my mother became frantic. My mother kept after my father to try and find him. He did nothing. A few months later Bobby called the 800 number where I worked. Bobby said he needed money for food. When I asked where he was he just babbled, like a Bob Dylan song, I could barely understand what he was saying.

I finally agreed to wire him money at a specific Western Union office in the morning. Then, thinking it over, I decided to drive the two hours to the location in person and see what was going on with him.

Once I spotted him, I opened the car door and asked him to get in. At first he was hesitant, "come on Bobby, I have your money lets go get some breakfast."

Bobby was tugging at his hair and rocking in the passenger seat. I was scared, either he was high on drugs or worse, it crossed my mind that he was having a mental breakdown.

When we arrived at a restaurant, Bobby was rambling. He started talking about how much he missed mom and Patricia. Then he turned the discussion to people from outer space.

Convinced he was not on drugs, I decided to talk him into returning back to Chicago. I was able to persuade Bobby to return to Chicago with me. Once at my apartment I sent Bobby into the bathroom for a shower and I made calls reaching out to those I knew in the medical community for help. I called mom to let her know he was okay and with me. Later that day a clinical psychologist I knew agreed to come over and assess Bobby's situation. By the end of the evening, after exhaustive talking, Bobby agreed to go with him for help.

We would later learn Bobby had been diagnosed with manic depression and schizophrenia. A few days after being in the hospital Bobby checked himself out and disappeared again. I was confused at the time how this could happen. If he was so sick why would he be allowed to voluntarily check out? Apparently, after 72 hours, if you're an adult, a mental health facility can't hold a person and make them stay for treatment unless they prove a danger to themselves or others. My mother was frantic and my father refused to accept Bobby's medical condition. His response was that the doctors were wrong and Bobby was fine.

I started dating a guy, and soon our relationship became serious. Mark and I spent a lot of time together hanging out at his place in the country.

My mother loved him even before she met him in person. Once she found out he was Jewish she was thrilled for me. She said, "Jewish men make the best husbands!"

Anytime a conversation came up between Mark and me about my childhood though I changed the subject. If Mark knew about my past I believed he wouldn't like me.

I believed I was damaged goods. I didn't want to be defined by circumstances beyond my control. People didn't speak of family violence, I thought. Painfully, I recalled how others reacted—the nun, teachers, school principals, even strangers—when I attempted to talk about my father, the monster.

Mark and I were inseparable. A few months after we started dating Mark was talking about marriage and buying a home together closer to the city. It wasn't long before Mark proposed and I accepted.

Did I have a clue as to what marriage was suppose to be? Absolutely not! Did I love him? I did love Mark, but not enough to trust him with my shameful secrets. I wanted Mark to love the strong, confident, successful, and loving woman that was going to be his wife. My past had no place in our lives. I couldn't change events, so why bother making it a topic of discussion?

We were married during a small private ceremony by a judge in the living room of our new home in a suburb forty miles outside the city of Chicago.

Mark continued to ask when I planned to have my parents over for dinner. He'd already met my mother and was anxious to meet my father. Frankly, I didn't want my father in my home.

My mother said it was important for her "well being" that I keep the peace.

My father wanted others to view him as a kind and caring man. I think he was worried I would tarnish his shinny hero image. If it were not for my mother's persistence, I never would have allowed my father into my home.

A few months passed and reluctantly I invited my parents to dinner. The sight of my father, as he walked through the front door of my home, turned my stomach into gut wrenching knots. I barely spoke five sentences to him all evening.

When my parents finally left and I was cleaning up after dinner, Mark said, "You were rather cold tonight to your father. I've never seen you so tense. I think he's a great guy. I enjoyed talking to him. Maybe you can try to patch up the relationship, Susan? It's clear you're holding on to stuff from when you were younger. Now that the two of you are adults ..."

I interrupted Mark in mid sentence, "What you witnessed from the moment my father walked in that door and shook your hand was an act. My father wants everyone to see and believe he's a great man. But, Mark, he's an evil and a dangerous man."

Mark shot me a look as if to say, you're a crazy woman. "Susan, maybe when you were growing up he was strict ruling your house with a firm hand. But what kid doesn't think at one time or another parents are mean in one way or another? But, Susan, that was a long time ago. I think it's time you work on forgiving him for whatever you remember him doing. He's obviously a different guy today. I'd like to get to know him, maybe I'll invite your father for a day of fishing on the boat or plan a day at the shooting range. Okay with you honey?"

It was not alright with me, but I was plum exhausted from having a conversation that was going no place.

I managed a half smile before responding, "Yes, that's fine with me."

Chapter Eight
Message from Heaven

My grandmother Carolyn came in from Florida to visit me for a few days. She didn't look well, her bright, rosy complexion had been replaced with a grayish pasty tone.

I'd known for sometime Grandma Carolyn was sick. She'd made arrangements while in town to visit and stay with Mark and me for a few days. Instinctively I knew she was dying.

For a brief moment, as she gazed into my eyes, I caught a glimpse of a sparkling light, what I believed to be a person's way of signaling their departure into the next life with God.

My husband and I made plans to take a cruise over the Christmas holidays. I joked with my mother before leaving that if anyone dies, they will have to wait until I come back home for the funeral. Two days into the cruise my mother called my office, trying to reach me in a panic, asking if anyone knew what cruise ship I was on. During dinner an officer on the cruise ship handed me a telegram.

It said, "Call your office or mother's house. Urgent." We were docked at an island without access to telephone service. Once the ship returned out to sea, the ship's captain arranged for a land line call. When I reached someone at my office I was informed my father was in critical condition, in a coma, and not expected to live.

My reaction to the news was pure joy. It meant my mother would finally be free to live her life. No one could understand my unwillingness to leave the ship and take a flight home, especially Mark.

He insisted we get off the ship at the next port and return. When I explained there was nothing we could accomplish by ending our trip, the decision was easy.

I continued to enjoy my vacation, in fact, a tremendous weight felt lifted off me. Finally, my father would not be able to cause anymore pain and suffering to my mother.

Upon my return home, I called my mother, surprised to learn my father was still alive.

She reported, "Your father suffered a massive stroke. He's been in a coma for several days. How about coming to the house this afternoon to pick me up, and we can meet with the doctors?"

I hesitated before telling my mother that was fine, but it was not. I was not okay wearing the concerned family member mask.

We met with the doctors. They didn't hold much hope for my father's recovery, even suggesting to my mother she begin making funeral arrangements.

As she and I headed for the elevator, up to the ICU, my mother's eyes welled up with tears.

"What's wrong?" I asked.

"You're going to think I'm crazy."

"Mom, just tell me, what is it?"

"I still love your father, even after everything he's done to all of us. We've been together a long time. Maybe I was holding out hope that he'd change. Until all this happened, I didn't think I cared anymore. But I do."

To say I was surprised was an understatement. I was in shock, and no, I didn't understand how she could still love him.

The block letters on the hospital door to my father's room, read, "Murphy, Phillip." I swung open the door. A nun was sitting vigil at his bedside praying over him. There he was, curled up in a fetal position, his wrists tied to each side of the bedrail so he couldn't pull out the intravenous tubing or wires from the machines.

His face was swollen, double its size, and his facial expression resembled a child, sleeping peacefully. The way my father looked, lying in the bed, like a helpless baby, was disturbing. Here was this macho man, now reduced to being a helpless child.

The nun asked who I was, explaining my father's fragile medical condition.

"The reason his hands are tied is because your father continues to have seizures and he thrashes in bed trying to remove everything to which he is connected. Oh, he has no idea. It is not intentional. We see this with patients who have suffered trauma to the brain. I've have been praying, asking God for a miracle. Many of the sisters from the rectory have been taking turns sitting vigil with your father. Sisters Anna and Elizabeth have known your father for many years. You, too, my child, must pray for a miracle."

"Ha! Yeah right," I thought to myself, "God should answer my prayer for once and let this man die."

"Thank you, sister. Could you please come back a little later, and if my mother is in the hallway, please ask her to come in," I replied.

"Why certainly. It was nice to meet you." The sister left.

I stood over the bed, staring at my father, watching as the machines in the room kept my father alive.

My mother walked in. "I should have told you what to expect."

"No, that's silly. I'm fine. Do you want to stay for awhile? What would you like to do?" I asked.

"I don't need to stay. Why don't we have lunch someplace and stop back on the way home?" she replied.

"Great idea, Mom. Let's go." Off we went to a restaurant.

I waited until we were seated at the restaurant. I was not comfortable with any of this, from the nun's words of wisdom to my mother professing to still love and care about my father.

Before I inserted my foot in my mouth, I asked my mother to explain what happened the night of the stroke.

"Well, I thought your father was drunk, but he wasn't. He fell on the floor in the bedroom and was having what looked like a seizure. I called an ambulance, and they took him to the hospital.

After the doctors examined him, they came out to the waiting room and spoke with Patricia and me. The doctor wanted to know if your father drank, because they could not figure out what was causing the stroke and seizures. I responded no, but Patricia got up from her seat and told the doctor, 'Yes. He drinks.' Your father has been in the ICU since he arrived. I was called to the hospital twice, watching and listening as a priest administered your father last rites."

"Mom, do you think you're feeling guilty, because maybe—just for a moment—you wanted Dad to die?"

"Oh, I'm not sure. Your sister was so upset with me for not telling the doctors immediately when I was asked if your father was a heavy drinker. I just don't know."

"Mom, with all due respect, remove that head of yours out from your behind. Are you forgetting how many times he sent you to the hospital, how he talked about killing us and burning down the house? What about the day we were pulled from the bus? He brought you home and raped you, not to mention how he almost killed you. I'm not sorry. I wish he were dead. There. I said it. Because then I would know for sure you'd always be okay and I wouldn't have to worry about you, And just so we are clear, don't expect me to return to the hospital for a visit or lend a hand if and when he recovers. When we leave here I'm dropping you off at the house. I have to go back to work tomorrow."

Yes, for the first time I was upset with my mother. After all we'd been through I couldn't fathom my mother's sudden change of heart. I'd thought of my father as a vicious dog who needed to be put down, otherwise he'd continue on his path of destruction. As long as my father remained alive, I believed he posed a serious threat to all of us.

That night, Grandma Carolyn passed away. The following day the doctor said my father's condition had improved dramatically during the night. The doctor told my mother he had witnessed a true medical miracle. It crossed my mind that my grandmother died so my father could live. I really believed her death allowed her son, my father, to live. My belief was based solely on a feeling. Sounds crazy but when my grandmother died I awoke from a deep sleep. I had dreamed that my grandmother was talking to me, stroking my hair and saying goodbye. And she asked me not to be angry with her for asking God to give her son another chance.

The very next day, mother called me at work announcing my father was out of danger. The doctors expected him to recover from his stroke.

I was so upset by my mother's news, I signed out of work for the remainder of the day. Walking around the streets of downtown Chicago thinking, how this was possible? Why is my father allowed to live? I wandered the city until it was time for me to catch the train home.

My father, on medical leave with full pay from the police department, was transferred to a rehabilitation facility specializing in the care of stroke and accident victims.

It was a brutal year for my father. He had to learn how to speak, feed himself, and walk again. With the medication my father was taking he was not supposed to drink. In the hospital he ate a minimum of half of a box of chocolates a day as a replacement for the alcohol he was not drinking.

When the medical facility asked to meet with family members to discuss my father's recovery process I refused to attend. My mother was convinced that my father was not capable of harming her any longer. I disagreed.

A year after the stroke he was released and sent home. My mother waited on him around the clock. When he got better, he began drinking again. My mother returned to work. My father called her constantly and followed her everywhere.

The combination of booze and medication made him unpredictable. I was concerned for my mother's safety. There was no one person I could confide in, not even my husband. Based on experiences going back to when police officers arrived at my home and they didn't arrest my father. I felt alone. I was certain Mark would treat me no differently. Maybe he would say I was exaggerating. I was scared he wouldn't want me anymore. I still believed that I was damaged goods. I believed the horror and shame of my upbringing to be my problem.

Just as I feared, my father began hurting my mother again. His verbal threats, one day while I stopped at the house, sent me over the edge. I heard him say to my mother, "don't even think of leaving me Roberta, I'll hurt ya."

Since I believed there was no one to talk with about this, not even my husband, I had to make a painful decision. I believed my mother's life was more important than my marriage. I decided if I was going to keep her alive, that meant moving nearby.

I knew Mark would not want to move, but I never gave him a chance to have any input in the matter. I wanted to give my mother more time. In my gut, I always believed my father was going to kill her. All I wanted was to buy my mother more time to live her life. My mother's life was worth more to me than anything in the world.

Unfairly, without any reasonable explanation, I filed for divorce. When my mother learned of my plans, she could not understand why.

"Mark is a wonderful man. He loves you. Why are you doing this?" my mother asked.

"Let's forget about it for now. What's done is done."

I had to carefully plan my mother's move out of the house. My mother was reluctant to leave until my sister finished high school. She continued to buy time with excuses as to why she could not leave. Finally, after a gun accidently went off in the house, my mother agreed to move out. A few months later I helped my mother find an apartment. Although Mark and I were divorced, he helped move my mother into an apartment within two miles of my parent's house. My sister had a few months before she finished high school and it was important to remain in the area close to her school.

Within a year after my divorce from Mark, I began dating again.

My job required me to travel between New York and Chicago. When I was in Chicago I stayed with my mother and sister.

My father began stalking my mother at work, the apartment, where she went to have her hair done, as well as calling her at all hours of the day and night.

This went on for nearly a year before my parent's divorce was final. In May of 1988, they were finally divorced. For the first time I would see my mother actually happy, making plans for the future and watching her discover a whole new world.

At the same time, my father's dangerous behavior increased to the point of obsession. I wanted to believe he would leave her alone after the divorce, however, he grew increasingly obsessive and angry. He left handwritten notes stuffed inside the lobby of the apartment building pleading for her to return. The telephone calls continued, between ten to fifteen daily voice messages on my mother's answering machine, ranging from: what a piece of selfish trash she was, to threats of, "it ain't over yet."

Stalking her apartment became a daily pattern. He parked in the back lot or across the street at the gas station, watching to see if she was going straight home from work.

When I sought help from the police department I was sent away by the desk sergeant as though I were the crazy one. I heard the officer laughing until I reached the front door. My father was still a cop, although technically he was on medical leave, he was just a few months away from his official retirement. I was told there was nothing anyone could do, he had not committed any crime.

Despite my father's behavior, my mother was happy to be free of him. She had her stomach stapled to lose weight. My mother was taking better care of herself. She looked great.

Around this same time I remarried. Jeff was completely the opposite of Mark. We'd met through a mutual friend one evening at a popular drinking establishment. From the moment of our introduction we locked eyes. Jeff was exciting in a reckless, bad boy sort of way and lots of fun to be around.

We had an instant attraction, like a magnet to metal. His eyes were the color of a deep blue sky and he had the body of Adonis.

Obviously I allowed my emotions to rule my heart. I had no business marrying again so quickly after I'd divorced Mark but I was searching for normal, whatever that was, but I hadn't a clue. And I'd asked my mother not to tell my father I'd remarried.

My sister was also preparing for college in Tampa, Florida. Our lives were all on track, or so I thought.

My father called me over the Christmas holiday, wanting to get together. I told him when I returned from out of town we could meet for breakfast somewhere. On January 14, 1989, I met my father at a pancake restaurant.

He didn't seem right to me. He was acting strangely, and I knew, from years of knowing him, that he was lying, trying to cover-up something by using words that didn't make sense.

"This is the first Christmas I have spent alone since your mother and I married. I don't know what I did wrong. I love your mother, and now she tosses away our life, after all I did for her. I gave her everything I had," he said, shaking his head.

I let my father have it. I said everything I'd always wanted to say, "Are you living in a fantasy world? Do you remember how you beat her almost daily when Bobby and me were kids? You treated and spoke to her using language unfit for a human being. Do you remember the day you took us off the bus, and raped her, and nearly killed her with your bare hands? Do you remember any of this? Huh, do you remember?"

My father's eyes welled up with tears. "I'm so sorry. I'd do anything to get her back."

"You're sorry?" I said. "Not allowing her to get a driver's license, or go to work? For as far back as I can remember, you told her you would kill her if she didn't listen to you or ever decided to leave."

My father attempted to speak.

"Shut up!" I continued, "I'm not finished! Do you have any idea what you've done to me, your own daughter? I'm clueless as to what a "normal" relationship is. My world's been filled with the fear you deposited like money in a bank account, dumping it directly into my life."

My hands were trembling. I was so angry I could barely sit still in my seat. "You were alone this past Christmas. I have always been alone, left to wonder what you'd do next. You hijacked my childhood. You son of a bitch you raped me! Do you have any memory of that? You took my life away because you were too busy drinking and holding us all hostage with your violent mood swings. You did this all by yourself."

We sat together for another hour, all the while I continued to speak to him in a disrespectful tone. I was so angry at my father who was trying to explain himself.

I had so much anger to release, but I also knew he had a handgun tucked in his side pant pocket. I noticed it when we sat down. I didn't want him to see or smell my fear and I had to think quickly to make an undetected exit.

I looked down at my watch, realized how late it was and made an excuse to go. The thought crossed my mind that he could pull out his gun and shoot me so I decided to do the unexpected— awkwardly, I stood up, kissed him on the cheek, and left.

It felt wonderful to have finally said and unburdened myself about everything this man had done to me.

I felt a sense of danger coming from my father, and I was not sure why. I also had a feeling this was to be the last time I would ever see him again. I cannot explain how I knew, I just did.

My marriage to Jeff quickly changed when I was called in to talk with a banker friend of mine who asked me to cover a bounced check Jeff had both written and cashed that was not his. If I didn't cover the check the bank was prepared to file criminal charges.

Upon further investigation I would learn Jeff had bounced checks all over the city with people I knew. That same day the doctor's office called with the news I was pregnant. Later that evening, I got in touch with Jeff asking him to meet me at our loft in the city. When he arrived, there was a moving crew taking my furniture out as I was packing my clothes.

"Susan, what's going? What the hell is all this?"

"You sir, are a con man. I just spent the entire afternoon writing checks out so they wouldn't haul your ass to jail. I can't believe you actually bounced a check to the restaurant where we held our reception after we got married. Those people are my friends! Not to mention all the others who cashed your stolen bogus checks."

I didn't tell Jeff the news about the baby. Every time Jeff attempted to explain, I replied, "Buddy, this party is over, there's nothing to discuss. I will have a lawyer draw up divorce papers and you'll have them at the end of the week." Temporarily, until I decided where to land next, I moved into a friend's home in the suburbs that he maintained when in town on business.

It was nearly midnight when I settled in for the night. My head was doing somersaults with everything I needed to do next. That included talking to my mother about coming with me and helping after the baby was born.

I had to be in New York on business early the following morning. I called my mother to warn her she needed to steer clear of my father and shared the news she was going to be a grandmother.

She called me the morning I was leaving, telling me my father wanted to talk with the two of us at the house. When she told me this, I had a sick feeling come over me.

"Oh, no! There's no way!" I blurted, "I'm not going over to that house. And neither are you mom! Stay away from him until I return from New York."

I took the first flight out of O'Hare airport and was in New York by 8:00 AM. My schedule was jammed with back-to-back meetings, but I couldn't concentrate. I had a bad feeling about my mother. Finally at mid-day I rose in the middle of a business meeting, excused myself, grabbed my coat and purse, and hailed a cab to the airport, hoping to get on the next flight back to Chicago.

By the time I landed and rented a car it was around 6:30 PM. I drove from the airport straight to my mother's apartment.

My mother was not at home. I thought it looked as though she would be right back. All the lights were left on in the apartment. I waited for about an hour.

Something was wrong. I contacted my maternal grandmother, and asked if she had heard from Mom. She told me no.

I left her apartment to go over to my father's house, however, I ended up clear across town for some reason. I was exhausted. I didn't feel like driving all the way back into the city to investigate. So I drove home, went to sleep and had the strangest dreams about my mother visiting me in the form of an angel.

That morning I called my mother's house, leaving messages on the hour to call me right away, I also called her place of employment, I was told she was away from her desk. I should have been reassured, but I wasn't. I needed to hear her voice. Mentally I was in a fog, losing track of time. It was near the end of my mother's work day when I called her office again and demanded to speak with her boss.

I was told my mother had not shown up for work that day. By this time I had driven to a friend's house nearby and asked for a telephone book.

From her kitchen table I started calling around to area hospitals. It was nearly midnight when I finished calling nearly every hospital and police department throughout the state. Call after call I was told no one fit her description.

I sat at the table trying to figure out where the hell she could be? Then it struck me, a feeling, somehow I knew she was dead. I realized the other person I'd not been able to reach and the only place I hadn't checked yet was my father's house.

My vehicle was blocked in the driveway by my friend's car. Not having any time to spare, I grabbed my girlfriend's car keys and announced, "I have to go to my father's house, he killed my mother."

My friend was startled and wanted to go with me but I said no. I had to do this alone.

As I turned the corner on Highland Street, my mother's yellow car was parked a few doors away from my father's house. I knew this wasn't good. With my car still running I threw it in park as it sat in idle in the middle of the street to investigate.

I had been correct.

After most everyone from law enforcement had left the house, Barbara, the neighbor who had been so helpful, asked me to come back in with her when I was finished.

Flaherty and another cop were still hanging around when I returned next door.

Barbara handed me a freshly brewed cup of coffee, "Susie, what about your sister, do you have a way to reach her?"

I thought for a moment who to contact. Patricia was away in Florida attending college. I was able to recall her number. One of her roommates, Angie, who was her best friend and also from a police family, answered the phone. She was half asleep. "Angie, Angie it's Susie, Patricia's sister, I need you to listen to me this is very important, you need to wake-up."

Right away Angie wanted to wake Patricia, "No, no," I stated firmly, "please, you can't do that." I still had not told her why I was calling. "Angie go splash some water on your face, get a pen and paper." When Angie came back on the phone she sounded more alert.

"Angie, you can't scream and I promise this isn't a dream. Listen to me very carefully, my mom has died." Angie was confused and started asking a lot of questions. Without me knowing it, Patricia had picked up a phone extension. I then added, "and, um, our father killed her, she's gone."

From her end of the phone I heard a piercing cry as Patricia screamed hysterically.

I made arrangements to have Patricia and Angie take an early morning flight to Chicago. The girls were joined at the hip throughout their years at a private Catholic, all-girls high school. People knew that where Angie was, Patricia was never far behind. As a result of their friendship, Angie and my mother were extremely close. Angie was treated as though she were her a third daughter.

A police detective from my father's unit would be at the airport to pick them up and bring the girl's to my mother's apartment. When Patricia arrived, I had a phone in each ear, fielding calls from friends, neighbors, and my father's colleagues while gathering paperwork to bring to the funeral home. It was chaotic to say the least.

I made some tea and we talked. Patricia had so many questions for which there were no immediate answers. I had Angie call her mom to pick her up so Patricia and me could be by ourselves for awhile. The alone time was brief as we were constantly interrupted by friends stopping by to offer their condolences. Somewhere in between all of this I forgot to call my grandmother and update her with what was going on.

The conversation with my grandmother was another project in and of itself. When she realized her daughter was gone she began barking orders at me on the phone—do this, and get that, come get her, call so and so ... it was too much.

There was a lot to do in a short period of time, including trying to locate my brother Bobby. I was already exhausted and barely able to hold a conversation. News of my parents' deaths traveled fast because the killing was broadcast on a popular news radio station. Jeff called my mother's apartment to see if I was alright. Within the hour, he was at the door. "I'm here to help, what can I do?" Jeff asked.

I looked at him not knowing how to respond. He started to speak, "Before you say anything, we're still married, you're my wife and your carrying my child." I looked at him questioning how he found out?

"While I was cleaning out the loft this morning, your doctor's office called, they heard about what happened on the news and the doctor is worried about your pregnancy. He wants you to call his office."

I made a list of various errands, sending Jeff out for awhile. Patricia cried with the news that I was pregnant. "When were you going to tell me about the baby?"

"Are you kidding me? I snapped back. "In the last seventy-two hours I received the news I was pregnant, kicked Jeff out of my life, and made arrangements to move out of the loft apartment. I was in New York on business, came back and found our parents dead. I had to make arrangements to get you and Angie here and now I'm trying to locate Bobby and finally, I've got to plan a funeral!"

Patricia screamed back, "it's always about you! When I'd call and talk to mom all she wanted to tell me about was Susie's going here and Susie's doing this, blah, blah, blah, I'm sick of it. You got to have mom longer than me. She loved you the most."

When I tried to comfort Patricia she pulled away and went into the bathroom. I walked over to the bathroom door, "Patricia, I'm sorry, but I've got to run out, there's a set of apartments keys on the kitchen table. I know your hurting and upset, but don't take it out on me. Take a shower, or something, I'll be back in about hour."

I decided to go to the doctor. When I arrived the nurse took me to an examining room. The doctor had known me for many years. He was also my mother's OBGYN. I undressed and waited.

"I'm very sorry about your mom, Susan. Let's check you out first, then get dressed and we will go to my office and talk."

I changed back into my street clothes and we talked. The doctor was concerned, because of the tremendous events and shock to my body, if I would carry the baby to term. The doctor was against giving me any sleep medication during the first trimester. I was really hoping to get a prescription. I hadn't sleep in days. The doctor gave me his home number and told me to call day or night, even if I couldn't sleep and just wanted to talk.

When I returned to the apartment Patricia apologized.

I had an officer from my father's unit attempt to track down my brother. When the police were unable to locate him, I called around to every low-income facility in Chicago.

I located my brother in a hotel, or flop house as it is referred to, for men. I contacted detective Tom Flaherty to go with me. The area was not safe for me to go to by myself and Flaherty offered to go with me once I'd located Bobby. Regardless of our differences, both Flaherty and I understood this was about Bobby.

We paid a visit to my brother. I learned he'd been living on the streets for over six years. Sometimes he had enough money to stay in a low income hotel. But when he didn't have any money he slept under a city street bridge.

Bobby looked similar to those whom I had served thanksgiving dinner at the church when I was a teenager. His blond hair was matted. When Bobby extended his hand to Tom, I noticed they were covered with blisters and scabs. Having Flaherty at my side helped me break the news to Bobby.

We could barely make sense of Bobby's conversation. In response to the news Bobby said he knew when we showed up something had to be really bad. He rocked on a stool, tugging at his hair. He never once looked at us.

I asked him if he really understood what happened? Bobby jumped up, his face flushed with anger as if he was ready to tackle me. Flaherty grabbed him by the shoulders and calmed him down. Bobby jerked out of his grip, took two steps back, "Yeah man, thanks, thanks I, I, uh, understand, sorry, Susie."

Then he kept repeating, "Yeah, yeah, I knew it."

Before we left, I wrote down my phone number and gave him some money. I told Bobby I was picking him up the next day for lunch and to get some new clothes for the funeral.

When I contacted the funeral home to check if they had picked up the bodies from the morgue, I was told no. The funeral director said the morgue wouldn't release the bodies until a family member came down for a formal identification. I was livid. Why was I having to identify the bodies? Everyone at the crime scene knew both my parents. I was assured by the commander that night this would be handled.

Flaherty was behind this, I was positive. The only person I could think of to go with me was my-ex husband Mark. I was scared and didn't know what to expect. A few hours later Mark picked me up and we drove down to the city morgue. Once inside I had to show identification and sign some paperwork. A man with heavy alcohol on his breath walked us into a room. A voice over a speaker said they were ready to open the curtain. I kept telling myself this was all a bad dream, this couldn't be real.

The curtains opened. On a double slab table, as if my mother and father were sleeping together, their dead bodies were visible.

I could clearly see the large hole in my father's forehead from the gunshot. My mother was next to him. In skin tone color they were about as white as the sheet covering their naked bodies. I buried my face in Mark's shoulder. The voice over the speaker said my parent's names and asked if these two were them. Mark responded yes and immediately took me out of there.

If Flaherty's goal was to torment me, he succeeded. The sight of my parents in the morgue remained locked in my vision, regardless of whether or not my eyes were opened, or closed.

As the oldest child in the family the responsibility fell on me to put everything in place. Making the funeral arrangements turned into another major ordeal.

Grandma, Patricia, Angie, and me went to meet with the funeral director. This was a mistake. My grandmother began arguing about having both my mother and father waked for visitation in the same room.

Grandma leaned over the walnut desk, raised her index finger at the man, "do you know what happened? He murdered my daughter. A wake in the same room?! Burn that son-of-a-bitches body! I hope he rots in hell!" There was no calming the woman down. The funeral director suggested that because people knew them both it might be better to have the wake at the same time, in one room.

"We aren't having that murderer in the same room with my daughter!"

I interrupted and asked the funeral director if we should even have an open casket for my mother? Questioning whether or not her face could be presented in an open casket. Before he could answer, Patricia cried, "Please, please, yes, I want to see mama one last time and say goodbye." It was getting late. I suggested that maybe Grandma, Patricia, and Angie go select a casket for mom. I stayed behind and made the arrangements for both my mother and father.

We agreed they would be waked together, my mother's casket would be open, my father's closed. She would have a full funeral service, my father would be cremated. When the three of them returned they couldn't decide on the yellow or pink casket. I rolled my eyes and said, "Please, just decide and tell the man."

After another hour of selecting the music, service, prayer, and mass cards I dropped Grandma off at home and the girls and me returned to the apartment. After making the funeral arrangements I was a wreck.

Taking my brother out to get clothes was a unique experience. The salesperson in the first store we entered politely asked us to leave, so we went to a discount store. Trying to figure out what size clothes Bobby wore was a challenge. Not to mention, when I would put socks and underwear in the shopping cart. Bobby would take the items out, look at the price and say, "it's too expensive," or that he didn't, "need new underwear or socks."

"Bobby, be quiet," I said. "I don't have time to fool around. Stop looking at what things cost. You leave that to me."

Once we were at the cash register and the clerk rang up a final total Bobby was upset.

"No, no, what are you doing? That's way too much money. Take me to the Salvation Army store. We can get what I need there for a lot less money."

"Bobby, it's okay," I replied. As I drove back into the city, Bobby continued to talk about how I had spent too much.

"Alright, Bobby. Tomorrow you'll be picked up and brought to my house. I'll hold on to what we bought today and you can shower and dress at my house. Remember to be standing outside the building at noon."

The next day at the wake, hundreds lined up to pay their respects to both my parents, their caskets sat next to one another in the same room.

My maternal grandmother was having a fit. "How could you do this to your mother, resting in the same room as that murderer?"

"Grandma, it was my decision. Please stop your bitching."

In attendance were many police officers with whom my father worked with over the years. As per my wishes, my mother's casket was open and my father's closed. His was draped with an American flag over the top. I could not bear to see my father's face.

People close to my father were upset with me. I didn't have mass cards printed with his name on them, and when I announced I was sending the good Catholic man into a fire chamber to be cremated it was met with anger and resistance.

"You can't do this to your father. He was Catholic. Phil deserves a proper burial," said Tom Flaherty.

"I'm sorry, but I didn't feel it appropriate to have mass cards or a 'proper burial' for your buddy. He's lucky to be waked at all, much less in the same room as my mother!"

"Susan, you're making a mistake. Your father loved you and Roberta." Flaherty continued to ramble on about my father's decorated law enforcement career.

"Thanks," I said. "But, your buddy murdered my mother. Stay clear of me for the remainder of the evening." I walked away.

Every half hour I would go and make sure Bobby was alright. He sat in a large chair in the lobby, greeting people. What had happened didn't seem to phase him. He showed no emotion as though he didn't comprehend that both his parents were dead. Bobby was in his own world.

As if I didn't have enough drama for one day, I noticed a beautiful blonde woman in her mid-forties walk into the room and place a single white rose on top of my father's casket. Then leave.

I was talking with someone when my grandmother approached me. "Susan, did you see what that woman did? Who is she? Why did she come here? Why didn't she pay her respects to me?"

"Grandma, I don't know. This isn't the time or place to get upset," I replied.

"I demand to know what she was doing here."

"Alright Grandma, sit tight. I'll see what I can find out." I went outside to look for the woman, but she was already gone.

After a long day, my sister and me, along with several others returned to the apartment. The funeral was scheduled for 11:00 AM the next morning.

We all went to bed. That night, I had a dream about my mother. This is what I dreamed:

The sound of a loud whistling tea kettle on the stove woke me. "Susie, Susie," a voice called out to me.

I opened my eyes. My mother was standing in the doorway of the bedroom.

"Wake up, honey." She was wearing a light green colored robe. I attempted to scream out to the others.

"No one can hear you," said the voice.

"I need you to listen."

This is the last time I will see you, until it's your time. I want you to know I'm fine. Heaven is a beautiful place. You're going to be okay.

Promise me you will look after your sister. You have much to do. Don't be sad. Be happy for me. I love you with all my heart." She blew me a kiss and she was gone.

I didn't tell anyone about this dream. They would have thought I was off my rocker.

The pain inside my spirit briefly lifted after my mother's visit.

To this day, I have no doubt God sent my mother to say good-bye. It was the tea kettle that convinced me. When she could not wake me up, my mother would put water on the stove and let the tea kettle make that piercing, annoying sound. It was the only way to get my attention in the morning. So I was certain it was her.

It was the one and only time she appeared before me in a dream.

In the morning we returned to the funeral home. I asked Bobby if he wanted to go to the casket and say a final goodbye to mom, "no man, I just want to sit here." And he sat back in the chair just outside the room.

A procession of bag pipe's lined up along the wall at my father's casket. As the police bag pipe's played, officers in the room stood at attention. When the music stopped a police Chaplain stood at the front of the room, asking everyone to pray for this fallen police officer, detective Phillip Murphy. I was puzzled. Who had invited them? I looked over at Tom Flaherty. He shot me a look, a gotcha smile. He was behind this. I was not laughing. Flaherty was not going to get the satisfaction of seeing me upset either.

Chapter Nine
Discovering the Truth

A few days after the funeral, Patricia went back to finish up her semester at college. I didn't want her to go so far away, but I knew she needed to go and it was what my mom would have wanted. We promised to talk to each other often on the phone.

Jeff and I met to discuss the future. I don't remember saying we'd get back together it just happened. I knew being alone after all that had just happened was not in my best interest. I needed someone with me.

Bobby and me remained in contact throughout my pregnancy. Nearly every day I drove into the city to take him out to lunch. Bobby was so skinny, I was worried he wasn't eating enough.

Bobby was definitely getting better. He had someone to talk to and interact with almost daily. While we we're having lunch one day, out of left field Bobby asked, "Susie, why did you leave me there?"

"Leave you where?" I asked him in return.

"How come you didn't take me with you when you moved out?"

"Take you with me, what, to live?"

"Yeah," Bobby replied.

"I don't know. I guess I never thought about it."

And then I thought to ask, "Bobby, did something happen to you?" My brother didn't answer me intelligibly, he was talking mumbo jumbo again.

"Come on Bobby, you can tell me. Why did you want to come live with me?"

"To get outta there, for Christ's sake. Dad was doing all kinds of crazy shit."

"Okay, Bobby, calm down." I changed the subject. Bobby was getting angry with me. I dropped him off and headed for home.

The next day, before I picked up Bobby, I contacted his social worker, requesting they fax me a release form so I could talk with someone about my brother. I had Bobby sign a release form giving me permission to speak with his doctors and social worker from the state program where he was enrolled.

I was told by the doctors that without medication my brother was dangerous to himself and others. Bobby had lived on the streets for so long it was not likely he would ever be able to function within a normal environment. The doctors felt his childhood played a major role in his mental health problems and that I needed to be careful not to trigger him.

The doctors asked that I break off all communication with Bobby before my baby was born. Doctors could not predict what Bobby might do once the baby arrived.

I saw Bobby up until about a week before the baby was born. I told him I was moving to another state as suggested by his doctor. I made sure he would be alright and I said goodbye. I never revisited why he questioned me about leaving him behind. I didn't want to cut off my connection with my brother. I had witnessed real progress and it was painful to stop all communication.

During my entire pregnancy, I remained stuck in the pain of my mother's murder. Most nights I didn't sleep. Communication with friends and family stopped.

I was treated as though I had a contagious disease. The few times I would run into someone at the grocery store, or mall, I heard the same excuse. "I have to go," "I'm running late," or "We'll get together and catch up soon."

After my parents' deaths, friends and family didn't stay in contact. All the promises to get together, to come over for dinner, or keep in touch never materialized. It was a double edged sword. No one wants to be reminded about a senseless tragedy or discuss the person who has been erased from our lives. Fact is, no one knew what to say, or how to act around me.

For several months I would actually pick up the phone to call my mother and remember she was gone. I felt like I was walking around in a fog.

Sometimes I didn't leave my house for days. Everything from eating to taking a shower required all my strength. My grief remained a constant companion. One afternoon, I flipped around the stations on the television. A preacher was talking about God. He instructed the audience to open their Bibles to John 5:14-15: "And this is the confidence that we have in him, that, if we ask any thing according to his will, he heareth us: And if we know that he hear us, whatsoever we ask, we know that we have the petitions that we desired of him."

On the couch I pondered the preacher's words to his television audience. Everything I heard him say sounded like a foreign language.

The Bible says God gives us life. He knows what will happen before we do. Is it God's intention to confuse us with pain and questions that have no answers? Or is the power of the devil so intense it dilutes God's miracles from fully manifesting themselves in our lives. It was clear the answers to my questions would not appear in my time, but God's time.

Resigning from my position in a mid-size investment banking firm was a reaction to my grief. I wanted to punish myself for my mother's death.

My mother was gone and I was left behind, shattered. It reminded me of the story book character, Humpty Dumpty. I could not be put back together, in mind or spirit, again. Painfully, my future would reveal itself to be woven into a poorly constructed quilt of my past.

I knew after the birth of the baby my second marriage had little, if any chance of survival. I was a basket case. The person I was married to took advantage of me during my grief. Figuring I would never step foot in the home where my parents died, he sold everything, including the kitchen sink for extra cash. When I did return to the house I asked him, "Where did everything go?"

He said he was remodeling the house so it could be sold. It was not true. Items of value had began to disappear and Jeff was back to his old tricks.

He actually tried to make me believe I was going crazy, and he almost succeeded.

At the time I had a lot on my plate. My maternal grandmother was still alive and living in a five-story, walk-up building. Someone had to take her shopping and be available to run errands. I suggested she consider going to live in a retirement center. She blew up at me for suggesting such a place. Pointing her cane in one hand and waving the other around, she told me a tall tale.

"Your mother and I planned on moving in together after your sister Patricia went to college."

I responded with laughter. I knew she was lying. My mother and grandmother never got along well enough to ever become roommates.

"You're disrespecting your mother's wishes. At this moment your mother's turning over in her grave. How dare you disrespect me and suggest that I leave my home!" she said to me.

"Grandma, the Jewish guilt routine won't work on me. This week we're going to look at new places for you to live. I'm not leaving you here alone."

I didn't want to come over one day, open the door, and find her dead. I was about to have a baby and taking care of her would've been more than I could handle.

We fought about moving for weeks though. I finally found a beautiful new home for my grandmother. Grandma kicked and screamed until she moved into the place.

I understood why she didn't want to leave, but we all had to move forward with our lives.

I had hired a lawyer to file the paperwork for my parents' estates. Once I received the letter as executor, I went to the bank where my father had an account and a safety deposit box. Because I didn't have a key, the bank had to drill open the box. Inside there were at least six large legal pads filled with my father's scribblings. At the back of the box he had a dozen or more dated, labeled cassette tapes, an old antique gun and several other personal items. I needed a shopping bag to carry everything out. I could not have predicted all my father had planned in those writings and tapes.

Late for a doctor's appointment, I put the shopping bag of his items in the trunk of my car. My doctor was amazing, he always went the extra mile for me throughout my entire pregnancy—following up on plans, needs, examines—making sure I was healthy and prepared.

"Everything is great," said the doctor, estimating my delivery date for the middle of September.

On the way home I stopped at a bookstore, looking for any books on the subject of battered women. I started to think about how I could begin to help other women like my mother who'd been abused.

It was clear to me that people really didn't talk about abuse and battered women. I suddenly had this idea that maybe I could change the world and the lives of victims and their children.

I could only locate two books on the subject in the store. One was written by Leone Walker, (*The Battered Woman*) the other by a woman named Ginny McCarthy (*Getting Free: You Can End Abuse and Take Back Your Life*). It was clear that books on abuse were not a popular subject.

The next day, I researched the issue of battered women at the library. I wrote down the names and contact information to senators, women groups, criminal justice agencies, and researchers working in the area.

I began a letter writing campaign, requesting information from programs across the country. Each package I sent contained a certified copy of my parents' death certificates.

A week later I finally removed the shopping bag of my father's things from the trunk of my car. At some level I knew going through the stuff from the safety deposit box would disturb me. I emptied out the bag on the dining room table, wondering what was so important that my father felt he had to keep these items locked up in a safety deposit box.

I'm not sure which bothered me more, the fact that my father had written out detailed plans about carrying out my mother's murder, or reading how I was going to be executed at the same time.

He wrote: "I expect Susie to show up at the house after I shoot Roberta. Susie will come in through the back door. I'll wait by the stairs on the landing. Susie walks in, fire gun at head."

My father had written out conversations and made notes for almost seven months.

In another journal entry dated October, 1988, he said, "Susie has to be disposed of, just like Roberta."

My father listed dates and times he went to the shooting range so he could practice. He wanted to make sure his "aim was steady."

Reading what he wrote made me nauseous. This was my own father and in his handwriting were thoughts that I, his own daughter, needed to be taken out for the, "problems I caused him."

Next, I finally got the courage to listen to the 120 minute cassette tape I had taken from the recorder machine the night I found their bodies.

There was no machine to play the tape on inside so I went out to my car and played it.

He had been recording all incoming and outgoing telephone conversations using a special device he hooked up from an ordinary cassette player.

The second to the last call was him talking to my mother to confirm if she was still coming over to the house. He needed to get some papers to the realtor so he could list the house on the market. He told her he could not do this until she signed too. And then he asked if she could stop and pick up a bucket of chicken to bring over. He was hungry.

The final call was to someone about cancelling an appointment. There was a long silence on the tape, and then I heard my father answering the front door. I could hear my mother in the background talking about how cold it was outside before she entered the house.

It sounded like they were in the kitchen and by the tone of his voice he was already half in the bag.

I heard her say she wasn't staying, where were the papers to sign, and here's your chicken. She put the chicken on the counter and then there was a terrified scream, "No, no, Phil what are you doing!?"

Next, the sound of someone tripping or falling on the floor. My mother was crying, screaming for him to stop, to let go of her.

From the sound of things she either saw the gun or it was at her head. My mother was frantic. Several times I thought of shutting off the tape but I didn't. I began to cry as I heard her being thrashed about in the kitchen. You could sense the fear even when they didn't talk.

"How do you like your freedom Roberta, huh? What do you have to say for yourself now? You ain't so fucking free are you!"

My mother screamed, "Phil, No! No, listen I'll do whatever you want, we can work this out."

There was coughing and chocking sounds as if my mother were trying to catch her breath.

"I told you what I'd do to you Roberta, you were warned."

"No! No, Phil, No, Please Don't, "... then a Bang. The gun went off.

My father continued to talk to her after the shot was fired. "See Roberta, look what you made me do." There was a long silence. As if he'd stood and watched her until she was fully dead. Then I heard him laughing. "You did this, you didn't listen. Why are you staring at me?" he asked.

I figured she was already gone and her eyes were still open. Then my father said something about how she needed to stop staring and he didn't like it. Then he said, "that's better." That must have been when he decided to cover her face with the towel.

I could hear my father's heavy footsteps pacing in the house.

He was mumbling. I heard ice crackling and then ice dropped into a glass and the sound of liquid being poured. And he kept talking to himself but I could not make any sense of what he was saying.

There was approximately 45 minutes between the first and second shot.

I couldn't bear to listen to any of the other tapes I found in the safety deposit box, each marked and labeled by my father. I called a friend to pick up all the tapes so I couldn't be tempted to play them. The journals I packed in a box and put them in the far corner of a dark coat closet.

Six weeks after their deaths, I signed for a certified letter from the Cook County Medical Examiners' Office. Enclosed were both my mother and father's autopsy reports. I waited until returning home to read the entire reports.

The time of death, based on my mother's stomach contents, was between 7-9:00 PM. The date of death was listed as January 16, 1989.

Included in the report: "the female victim died of a gun-shot wound to the front of the face at close contact." My mother didn't die immediately according to what I read. She had no brain activity, but she had probably remained alive for several hours after being shot.

That made sense. My father's partner, Tom Flaherty, said my father probably covered my mother's face with a towel after he shot her.

It made me sick as I thought of how my mother might have suffered.

Also included in the autopsy notes: "the male victim died instantly from a close, self-inflicted gunshot wound to the head." I studied every word on the reports for several hours.

The following morning, I paid a visit to Barbara, the next door neighbor, and asked her a few questions. I asked her if she knew who was home around 7:00 PM on the 16th of January, if she had heard anything out of the ordinary.

Barbara said she's heard what sounded like the backfiring of a car engine and that her dog was acting strange that night. What seemed like an hour or so after the first sound, she heard another. She added, "it was odd that the light in the kitchen was off, that light was always left on."

During my pregnancy, I kept busy researching the issues surrounding victims of violence and their families and clearing out what was left at my parent's house.

My father had burned or cut up documents and destroyed most of the family photos. I salvaged very little of our existence as a family. I made an appointment with a lawyer downtown. He agreed to take my case, filing legal action against the City of Chicago and the

Police Department for allowing my unstable father to renew his gun certification as a law enforcement officer.

I was going to try and use my parents' deaths to change how the police department handled officer related violence in their own homes.

Soon after this, I received two greeting cards in the mail. Inside someone had written: "To my loving daughter, Susan." The other card was signed, "your loving father."

Someone had gone out of their way to scare me. If they were trying to send me a message, it worked. I was scared. Whoever sent the cards knew where I lived, which was not public knowledge. After my parents' deaths, I had all of my mail redirected to another location for safety reasons, so I knew the cards had to be from someone within the police department.

Without providing an explanation, I told my lawyer to drop the lawsuit. I realized if I was going to take on the issues of domestic violence and officer involved abuse in the home I'd better have a plan to include my own personal safety. I was about to publicly expose the silent, blue brotherhood of the badge.

During those summer months, instead of happily preparing for the birth of my child, I buried myself in law books and researched information about abuse.

I was going to change how the world viewed family violence in the same way my mother had.

Chapter Ten
Running on Empty

While engaged in my research on abuse my water broke. I was in labor. My husband contacted the doctor and we went to the hospital. I had requested an epidural and was laying on my side, having contractions, when the anesthesiologist and the nurse came in to my room.

I was surprised to discover that the anesthesiologist was a woman. I was told to lay still as they administered my epidural. Listening to them converse, I learned that this doctor also had a daughter by the name of Susan. The doctor called her, "Susie."

I always cringed when my mother called me Susie in public. I never liked being called that.

The doctor made references to her daughter and it felt like I were listening to my own mother carry on about me with a complete stranger.

Coincidently, I was the same age as this doctor's daughter "Susie."

The anesthesiologist rolled me over on my back. With a look of surprise, she remarked that I even looked just like her daughter and said, "but I can tell you, she wouldn't make as good a patient as you. She doesn't do well in the pain department."

The anesthesiologist laughed, similar to my mother and I wondered if I were imagining all of this? Was my mother standing with me now? The doctor's facial features were identical to my mother's. Through the surgical gown, I could see, she had the same love for food as my mother.

The doctor was short and waddled when she walked. A calm warm feeling draped over my body. The labor pains subsided. I sincerely felt as though my mother was in the room with me.

My mother and I had often discussed the day I would give birth and how the experience of a new life would change me forever. My mom hoped to share this moment with me when and if the day arrived.

My mother often referred to childbirth as, "God's blessing."

Finally I was wheeled into the delivery room. I could not help but stare at the doctor. When she caught me looking at her, she smiled at me, patted my hand and said, "It's okay, dear." Although I couldn't see my mother, I felt her warm presence in the room with me as I was delivering the baby.

My doctor was on one side and the anesthesiologist was on the other instructing me to push. I gave birth to a beautiful and healthy baby boy. His father and I named him Vincent Patrick. I thought I heard a voice whisper in my ear, "I'm proud of you."

After the delivery I felt the presence of my mother leave the room. I wondered if God allowed miracles to happen to people when they didn't pray or dwell over events in their lives. I certainly didn't expect to feel my mother's presence. Perhaps it was the drugs, but there were too many similarities to chalk my feelings off as mere coincidence.

I felt so good after giving birth, I asked my doctor if I could go home. He told me I needed to rest and "take advantage of the peace and quiet," because once I left the hospital with Vincent, my life would change.

Having a baby didn't bring our family closer. Jeff continued playing mind games. Items of value and money vanished. It turned out he was feeding a cocaine habit. My constant nagging only encouraged him to continue his bad behavior. I'm not proud of allowing this to continue, but I did so because my son needed a father, and I needed a family. Jeff would come and go as he pleased, without any explanation. When I was being released from the hospital, my son's father had been missing in action for two days, partying somewhere with friends. I stayed in the relationship because of the baby.

I believed carrying my son full-term under difficult circumstances was a sign from God. The first two weeks after I brought my son home from the hospital I would sit up close to the bassinet watching Vincent while he slept. He was so beautiful. I could hardly believe I'd given birth to this perfect child.

Six weeks later, my sister Patricia flew in from Florida for Vincent's christening. Our sisterly relationship continued to be a roller coaster ride of emotions. We would never recover who we once were as sisters, our relationship remained altered after our parents died.

Patricia was angry, in particular, about my desire to create a public platform to change society's understanding of abuse, stalking, and homicide.

"I'm embarrassed by what our father did and you want to shout it to the world? Susie, you're crazy damn it, let it go, they're dead! Take care of your new son and forget about what happened," she said to me.

"Patty, Honey, I can't forget. I kept mother alive all those years and now I'm going to do it for others in violent relationships like mom," I replied.

"Susie, what the hell is the point? She's dead! You can't bring back the dead! Nobody cares about what happened and you can't magically snap your fingers and change anything. Angie told me a couple of weeks ago about the lawsuit you filed against the Chicago Police Department. When the hell were you planning on telling me about that?! Angie said her father called and told her you need to reconsider going forward. This sort of stuff is gonna get you killed!" Patricia said.

"Patricia, I had the lawsuit dropped a couple weeks ago."

"Good, please drop all of this ridiculous nonsense, now!"

In between tears Patricia said she was worried about losing me.

I didn't buy it. She was angry and embarrassed with what I was publicly planning on doing.

We discussed the possibility of her moving back to Chicago. She was dating someone I felt was way too old for her. Patricia was nineteen years old. The guy she was seeing was thirty-four.

While she was in town I introduced her to boys her own age, hoping she would move back. I desperately wanted to repair our relationship.

During the first year of Vincent's life, I stayed home with him. In the second year, I made arrangements with a childhood friend's mother to watch my son in her home for a couple days each week. Within a month, Vincent was at the sitters daily. There was a real need for changing how the courts handled domestic violence cases. I sat in court rooms as if they were my classroom, soaking up everything I could as it related to the lives of victims and the law. I determined that the process for a court order of protection was doing nothing more than lip service, just a false sense of safety for victims seeking legal action against their abusers.

After speaking with some of the women in court, I saw how my voice, because of my mother's murder, could assist victims of domestic violence to be safe and remain alive. I started contacting local radio stations and talking about my parents' deaths and how we needed to treat domestic violence in the home as a criminal matter.

Jeff and me were like two ships passing. I ignored his activities for the sake of Vincent. I spent my days in domestic violence courthouses which looked more like an audition of, "Judge, please give me a court order of protection." The courtroom was filled. Women had to stand and wait outside, lining the corridors until the bailiff came out from the courtroom and called their names. More than half who sought orders of protection to document the abuse in their relationships were denied, often because of their ethnicity.

First a victim had to fill out paperwork that took two or more hours, and if she didn't have a police report number, she had no chance of obtaining a court order against her abuser. The process from downstairs, up into the elevator, was the first part to this circus-like procedure.

From the moment a victim entered the courthouse lobby it was mayhem. Once they made it past security they were to follow large green arrows directing them to a waiting room, as if cattle being branded. There she took a numbered ticket from a machine as though she were at a deli counter in a supermarket. Then she waited in the hot, overcrowded room for her number to be called out. At this point a clerk handed the woman a packet of paperwork to fill out in yet another room. Depending on the crowds this could take all morning. Finally she would go in the elevator and up to the assigned courtroom where they would find the floor wall-to-wall with victims waiting their turn. It was truly a circus-like procedure that continued until the victim was before a judge.

Getting into the courtroom all in the same day was difficult enough. Often these women had to take time off from work without pay. Many had to bring their children because they either didn't have day care or couldn't afford to pay someone to care for their children.

I watched for hours as judges either granted or denied orders of protection to victims. On a 5" x 8" notepad, which I kept in my purse, I would jot down inconsistencies in a judge's ruling as to why the court was denying an order of protection for the woman.

After a while, I realized some of these judges were responding out of ignorance, or taking advantage of how little these women knew about the law and their rights under the law.

I surmised that if I learned about the legal system, I could change these women's lives if I stood next to them before the judge. I could help them receive their court order of protection.

I joined a grass roots organization whose membership was made up of service providers for battered women within Illinois. Quickly, I rose through the ranks of the Chicago Metropolitan Battered Women's Network. An organization made up of forty agencies services for victims of abuse. I was appointed to the Board.

I joined committees. I studied law books at a nearby college library. When a judge refused to grant a woman an order of protection, often based on her appearance or the color of her skin, I would go and stand with the victim in the courtroom, often demanding to know on what basis the judge was refusing to grant a court order of protection. I always carried a large safety pin in my bra, often taking it out in front of a judge, pricking my finger, drawing blood and asking, "your honor we all bleed the same, the this victim deserves her order of protection."

Sometimes a judge would have the bailiff escort me to his chambers where I was ordered to sit until the judge got off the bench. Usually, I was scolded by the judge for pricking my finger in court and drawing blood.

I was also told I was too bold and disrespectful in the courtroom or that I had no business questioning why someone was not granted a court order of protection in his courtroom. If I really put up an argument with the judge, I was sent to a holding cell for a couple hours where I'd remain until the judge finished for the day.

The judge would walk up to the 8' x 10' lock-up area where I was sitting at the end of the day, put his index finger up to the bars and state, "Next time you embarrass me like that, I will throw you in jail. Do you understand me?" Then call for the sheriff to unlock the door.

I was not treated by the courts with kindness, but with intimidation. Over time, I was quickly labeled a thorn in the court's side, a trouble maker.

One morning I read in the newspaper that a woman named Betsy Miles had been shot five times in a downtown Chicago building by her boyfriend. She was in critical condition. The police had issued a statement that, "they were looking for the man, who was both armed and dangerous."

I felt I could do something to help the police find the man. I drove to the hospital. When I arrived at the woman's room I was surprised to see no one standing guard outside her hospital room. I was certain the boyfriend who shot her was going to return and finish her off.

I introduced myself to the victim's sister, who was reading the Bible to Betsy when I walked into the room. We left Betsy's hospital room and walked towards a row of chairs near the elevator and talked.

I always carried a couple sets of my parents' death certificates in my purse. Having official, notarized death certificates got people's attention. Plus, each certificate clearly stated the cause of death. This was a way to show people I knew what I was taking about.

When I handed the certificates to Betsy's sister, I explained how I believed I could be of service in bringing media attention to the case and possibly offer a reward for the boyfriend's arrest. I didn't have a specific strategy in mind, just a feeling I could help.

From Betsy's hospital bed, I called news reporters, explaining that she had been shot multiple times and yet had no security outside her door. The police were doing almost nothing to investigate the case because, in my opinion, Betsy was an African American victim.

Betsy was going to be permanently disabled. The doctors were unable to remove a bullet from her back. No one would say with certainty if she would ever fully recover. I scored no brownie points with the hospital press person, who was less than thrilled with me for contacting the media.

I made arrangements for my son to stay overnight at the babysitters and then I literally parked myself outside of Betsy's hospital room, pulling a chair from the nurse's station and sleeping outside her door in case the boyfriend showed up. Don't ask me what I would have done if he had showed up. I hadn't thought that far ahead. The next morning I left briefly, checked on my son, showered, changed clothes, and returned to the hospital.

I'd made arrangements with Betsy's family to offer a reward for information leading to the boyfriend's capture and prepared to hold a press conference.

I was required to get permission from the women's organization to do this if I wanted their endorsement. They agreed to attend in support of the victim, but they had little faith I could get the media to show up and cover the press conference.

I lucked out when the impossible happened. A half hour before I was to hold the press conference outside the door of the courthouse, I learned that the boyfriend had committed a murder five years prior in another state, for the exact same crime against another woman he'd been dating.

During the boyfriend's extradition across state lines, he had escaped from jail. After which he'd changed his name and moved to Chicago. With this information, I now had a breaking news story.

Both the local and national media were present for the news conference. I was able to provide information unknown even to the police or the State's Attorney's office. It was the first of many breaking news stories that followed.

Two days later, someone who'd watched the news spotted the boyfriend and contacted the authorities. The boyfriend was apprehended and charged with the attempted murder of Betsy. Afterwards, he was returned to the state from which he had escaped and stood trial for murder. The boyfriend received life without the possibility of parole. After this he was returned to Illinois to stand trial for almost killing Betsy.

I spent the next couple of years working similar cases for those whose cries for help fell on deaf ears, cases where women and their children would have likely died if I didn't intervene and help them through the complicated legal system and on with their lives.

The media played an important role in my work. Each time I called about a case, it was covered by the media. The State's Attorney's office was less than thrilled with my "rodeo show," the phrase they used when I was summoned to a meeting in their offices.

My life began to take shape during the day while my son was at the babysitter. I volunteered my time at the courthouse to help others. I had a talent for working on cases and providing strategies that kept women and their children from being killed. I really couldn't take the credit for any success because I felt more like an instrument God was using to make a difference to those who needed help.

The more difficult a case, the easier it was for me to provide a successful outcome. After all, I had one hell of a training ground as a child.

However, instead of being embraced by the women's agencies and the State's Attorney's office and police departments, I was seen as unwilling to be a team player. I was misunderstood because I would only do what was best for the safety of the victim's life.

People quickly forgot that I involved myself in this issue because my own mother was murdered. I thought my personal experiences would have greater importance, but it didn't seem to matter. The "system" wanted me off their backs. No one cared for the way I went about getting cases resolved, especially if a victim's rights under the law were being ignored. Often I contacted the media when the State's Attorney's office or police department messed up on a case, or if a victim's case was not properly handled. Repeatedly the blatant train wreck of the legal system resulted in a one way ticket for victims—the cemetery.

There was an urgency, under the current law, to do its job—to ultimately prosecute rather than offer the abuser plea-bargains, or issue charges that included little if any jail time, or just a slap on the wrist by a judge. These were real crimes and I expected them to be treated as such, not swept under the rug.

I met with a woman, Elizabeth, who wanted to start a domestic violence agency. She was also a current client to whom I provided advocacy.

Elizabeth had all the paperwork in place and she was looking at office space. I was running out of room in my kitchen. It was time to start an agency. The two of us opened our new office directly across the courthouse parking lot. I put up the funds required to get us started until we received grant money. There were days when my work went into the wee hours of the morning.

The importance of a daily routine was often a challenge, but I knew picking up my son early enough to have dinner and spend time together until his bedtime was important. My son's father would often be gone without notice, days at a time, coming and going as he pleased. Our relationship was non-existent as husband and wife.

I inserted myself in the lives of total strangers, jumping into situations the same way I had as a child for my mother, often with little, if any, regard for my own personal safety. Strategically I would figure out the steps necessary for a woman to leave her abuser.

The services provided ranged from finding legal representation, employment, housing (landlords donated apartments), medical services, and in cases where I felt a woman was going to be killed, a new identity and relocation services were provided. I was able to make it look like someone moved to Canada, when, in fact, they were closer than the abuser realized.

I planned ten steps ahead of the abuser's next move. After all, I'd had one of the best teachers, my own father. Cases were handled as they related to the abuser and the victim, no differently than a person's own DNA. A one size fits all approach was not effective for the population I served.

Strangers often commented on the street that, "I was doing God's work." I started to realize that something good was being born out of my tragedy. Maybe I'd unknowingly stumbled upon God's plan for me?

Still traumatized by the events leading up to my parent's deaths, I worked hard to maintain a tough as nails public image. But unconsciously, I remained the scared little girl trying to save total strangers and victims in danger.

I was the little girl who was unable to save her mother, now rescuing women and children as a way to make up for the pain and grief I continue to own and still carry from my childhood.

Busily I provided assistance and direction, I worked and worked tirelessly. I bathed in it, played in it, slept in it. Yet, in the end I lived with neither light, nor hope.

My happiness was wrapped like a pretty package giving hope to others and I passed it out like free food at a supermarket. I might as well have stood on a busy street corner with a bull horn in my hand shouting something to the effect of, "Hope here! Come and get your hope! All you have to do is ask."

I knew how to give it to others, but I didn't know where to begin when it came to myself. Hope, for me, was as foreign as understanding another language.

Most days I seemed to run on empty, I was so busy taking care of everyone else. At times I felt as though I was stealing the last ounce of strength inside me and handing it over as food for survival to those who needed it. Maybe I'd watched too many episodes of *Superman* as a kid. I certainly felt like Clark Kent as he changed into his costume so he could, "save the day."

When you constantly give pieces of yourself away and you don't recharge your own batteries, you begin to run out of steam. I was being driven by sheer will, determined, no matter how many hundreds of woman I spoke to across the county, to offer words of wisdom, Unfortunately I never knew when to say no.

Stopping at 5:00 PM never seemed to happen, instead I took what I referred to as "hiccup breaks." To the minute, I had my required daily routine down to a science.

I knew from the time I left the house in the morning how much I had to cram into my day. When court was over I'd pick up Vincent from the babysitter. We'd have dinner, play, prepare for bed and a story before he fell asleep. Then I would go back to answering calls from strangers in distress, or prepare cases for court the following morning. Rarely did I get more than two hours of sleep a night. I was living and playing in a dark sandbox, never stopping to deal with my pain or anger following my mother's death.

Since I didn't make time for myself my grief turned into a self-medicated exercise for which I became an expert, like a game of hide-and-go-seek. I believed the right to be happy belonged to others, not me. That it was something you earned, like a merit badge.

In my home, growing up, the act of survival was all I had known. Not once could I remember seeing the adults in my house happy or interacting as a loving couple. We were feed fear for breakfast, lunch, and dinner.

At the domestic violence agency, Elizabeth and I met with a company who wanted to provide free, armed guard security services for our "high risk clients," those we determined were in imminent danger. The new partnership with the security company included having my own personal detail of bodyguards.

The cases coming into the agency were considered dangerous, many involved police officers who had been violent in their own home, resulting in an officer being arrested, suspended, or fired from the police department.

I was becoming a potential target for those angry officers. The security company insisted on round-the-clock protection for me and my son. I was not allowed to drive. The security detail accompanied me almost everywhere, the only exception being when I went into the ladies' room.

With the new partnership also came more media coverage, from radio shows and talk shows, to magazine interviews and profile pieces in the local and national media. Within a year, I would pay the ultimate price.

I interviewed a number of lawyers in hopes of filing a class action lawsuit in federal court for the failure to protect victims of abuse. I had an idea that if I could clearly show how the legal system had failed a group of victims, similar to a class action filing, who'd barely escaped their abusive relationships with their lives, I could create a set of procedures: from police responses through the courts, which would actually save lives.

Once I found an attorney willing to take this case and file a class action lawsuit, the train to justice began. Five cases from our client list were chosen for the lawsuit. Each victim had been stabbed, shot, beaten, and left for dead by their abusers. In each case, prior to the incidents of abuse, the police had refused to make an arrest, an order of protection was denied, or vacated in court. Under the law each victim's right to protection had been violated.

Elizabeth and I prepared for the massive press conference. The morning of the conference the five women were instructed to meet at our offices an hour prior to the news conference. As the time to walk over to the Dirksen Federal Building arrived, Elizabeth was missing in action. She didn't answer her mobile phone and I panicked, thinking she had got into a car accident on the way to the city.

We proceeded without her. After the filing of the lawsuit we held our press conference with both local and national media in attendance.

The case would go on to be a ground breaking one for domestic violence victims and their children as to how both the courts and law enforcement responded to these crimes. Six months after filing the lawsuit, three of the five victims no longer wanted to participate and asked to be removed. When asked why, they didn't want to give an answer, or were too scared to say. I had a sense the victims had been *visited* and that's why they backed out.

At first, though, having filed the suit I was riding on a high cloud until I returned to my office, or what was left of it. All the furniture, files, and office equipment were gone. The office was completely cleaned out, as were all the agency monies. At the end of the day I learned Elizabeth had moved to another office, taking everything with her. When I finally reached her by phone, she said to me, "I told you not to file a law suit against the City of Chicago in federal court. But, no, you would not listen to me."

Immediately, I met with the same lawyer who filed the class action lawsuit. With help from the lawyer I set up another domestic violence agency. Which, by Monday, was up and running, it was named—Project: Protect.

Around this same time I was in the process of divorcing my son's father. On Tuesday of that week what I believed was to be an uncontested, mutually agreed upon divorce was suddenly not that at all.

My divorce was being contested. My son's father had a new and expensive attorney representing him. I wondered how he could afford a four-hundred-dollar-an-hour attorney from the largest law firm in town.

I was summoned to court on an emergency order for a change of custody filed by my husband's lawyer. I could not figure out for the life of me what was happening.

In court, both of our lawyers filed their appearances on our behalf. Immediately, the judge ordered the case sealed. The court determined I was a public figure, and it would not be in my child's best interest if people had access to our personal information.

The judge, without a hearing, granted the removal and temporary custody of my son to his father. I was devastated. It felt as if I had been punched and had the wind knocked out of me. It would take me a while to understand what had happened.

We left the courtroom, and I asked to speak with my son's father for a moment.

"Why are you doing this? We had an agreement."

He smiled. "*Had* as in past tense. We no longer have an agreement. All I'm going to tell you is watch your back. You've pissed off a lot of people who want to see you go down." He excused himself and left.

Everything began to add up. I presumed a deal was made between government officials and Elizabeth to shut me out of my own agency. I'd not only publicly embarrassed both law enforcement and the prosecutors, I'd cost the city a great deal of money, forcing the City of Chicago's corporation counsel office to pay out large settlements to victims and families.

Making sure both my legs were cut off, a deal must have been made with Jeff.

Later that day, I met privately with someone from city government, hoping they would be able to provide answers to my questions.

I was told, "You've not only embarrassed the city, you cost them a tremendous amount of money in assisting families by filing wrongful death lawsuits on their behalf. You've made a lot of enemies and people want you stopped."

"What are you talking about?" I asked.

"You heard me," said the city official.

"Who's behind this?" I demanded to know.

"I'm not at liberty to disclose details. I'll tell you this though, you better rethink how you're assisting your clients. Make sure you have release forms indicating you're an advocate, not a lawyer and have them signed by every single client. They're not finished with you yet. There are rumblings the State's Attorney has convened a grand jury to have you indicted for practicing as a lawyer among other issues. Lay low for awhile, Susan. I'd recommend you not do any media interviews either. Tighten your seat belt, I think you're in for a bumpy ride."

I thanked him for his time and left. Devastated, I went home and called the head of the security company to ask that they pull the detail off me until Monday. I wanted to be alone to sort things out.

I took a hot shower, to wash away the day. It did nothing. I paced back and forth in the living room asking God why this was happening?

Chapter Eleven
Water under the Bridge

"Why?" I asked myself, looking at my living room ceiling, half expecting it to cave in and fall down on me.

My divorce had turned into another war. I had no strength left to fight this battle. My son was now a casualty of the cruel and common tactics of power and control often used in divorce when one parent attempts to send the other out for slaughter. Quite simply, my son's father was angry with me when I filed for divorce.

We'd worked issues out, or so I'd thought, until the unexpected fire storm of recent events.

This experience was similar to the victims I provided assistance. Having to watch while abusers continued to victimize them and their children, because they were ending the relationship with the person.

My mental stability became a major issue before the judge in court, due to accusations from my son's father, citing that I had grown up in a violent household and my father had killed my mother.

"She's crazy!" his divorce lawyer claimed during the next status hearing in court while using newspaper articles and my parents' death certificates to make his point, waving them like a flag in front of the judge.

"Your Honor, we ask the court to consider the public life lived and led by the plaintiff. She speaks, lives, and breathes her parents' tragedy. We've all seen her work in the papers and on television for the cause of battered women. At this time we feel it is in the best interest of the minor child to ask that continued temporary custody be awarded to my client, until such time as Ms. Murphy-Milano can be seen by a psychiatrist to determine her fitness as a parent. Additionally, we have filed a motion with the court ordering a mental health evaluation," the lawyer declared.

"Your honor, I object. The only harm the respondent is doing to the minor child is denying access to his mother. If council is so insistent on a mental health assessment, then I respectfully ask the court for an evaluation on Mr. Milano," responded my lawyer.

I sat at the table with my attorney, stunned by the lies about me. My attorney had objected to the motion, saying there was no basis for the allegations the other side was presenting.

"Conveniently taking what my client does to help others is not a valid reason to deny visitation or remove custody. Your Honor, the respondent has manufactured lies, with no proof to back up these outrageous allegations," my attorney explained.

"It's best for the child that we err on the side of caution," responded the judge.

The judge ruled that both my son's father and I schedule mental health evaluations with a professional chosen by the courts. In the meantime, no decision would be made as to when I would be allowed to have visitation with my son.

The judge wanted to wait until after the mandated evaluations. I knew this process could take months. It was clear my son's father was angry with me for ending the marriage, and he was going to use Vincent to get back at me.

I felt was alone. I had similar feelings when my mother died. Gone, never to return, a death to my heart. My son had been ripped away from me. I knew where all of this was headed and I wanted no part of it. I was unable to fight both the legal system and, now, my son's father. Whoever was behind this master plan wanted me out of the way.

The manufactured words my son's father and his attorney used against me in court were like daggers thrown, with perfect aim, straight into my soul. Sighting an unrelated issue in a divorce proceeding and applying my parent's deaths made it seem as if the courts were saying murder was a genetic disease. Bottom line, if my father was crazy, therefore I must be too.

Again I thought about the motion to have the divorce file sealed. "The plaintiff is considered a public figure your honor with numerous connections to the media. In the best interest of the child, we respectfully ask the court to rule in favor of sealing the case."

My lawyer had objected, but the friendly eye contact between the judge and Jeff's lawyer, indicated that this discussion, to close-off the file, had been pre-arranged before what seemed a circus-like hearing.

When the judge said he didn't want the case tried in public and ordered a court seal, so went the chance of ever having Vincent back in my life. The legal system and the political machine were punishing me for refusing to play ball. The divorce was final, with custody issues to be revisited at a later date. Suddenly, I didn't feel worthy as a mother. I questioned my faith in the legal system and most of all in God. Without my son, there didn't seem much point in continuing to live.

The next day, I met with a Chicago divorce lawyer with whom I had struck up an immediate friendship. Her passion to help women and their children in divorce, custody, or abusive relationship was music to my ears. Jennifer Waters and I quickly embarked on a journey to help others.

Embarrassed by my personal situation with my divorce, I waited a few weeks before I asked Jennifer for help with my case. She agreed to represent me. I couldn't afford her fees in what would become a long drawn out court battle so we worked out an arrangement. I changed lawyers and was represented by someone within her own firm.

The Christmas holiday was approaching and I wanted to be with my son. Court was a disaster. This time, my son's father made accusations in court that I'd put a gun to my son's head and he was in fear for his life. I didn't even own a gun!

Once again, my son's father was throwing out anything that might stick to a wall. The judge ordered a series of supervised visitations be conducted to observe how my son and I interacted with one another. A court-appointed mental health assessment was to be submitted to the courts for consideration. This would not take place until after the Christmas holidays.

Jennifer's office filed an emergency motion with the courts so I could see Vincent for Christmas. I lost it in court. I started screaming at the judge, calling him every name in the book.

Finally shouting, "This is a set up!" and stormed out through the doors and into the hallway.

"Get back in there right now and apologize," demanded my lawyer.

"No, I won't. I'm not going to say I'm sorry. This has been going on for over a year." I got into the elevator and left the courthouse.

I turned off my pager and wandered the streets of downtown Chicago. I kept walking until I arrived at the bridge several hundred feet away from the Tribune Towers building. I stared at the icy cold water and thought how easy it would be to climb up on the railing and jump off.

The longer I stood on the bridge the better the idea felt. Suddenly, my mind thought of the movie, *It's A Wonderful Life* and the scene where Jimmy Stewart jumps off a bridge and is rescued by an angel, ultimately saving his life. "Ridiculous to think an angel is going to rescue me," I thought to myself.

Weighing my options, I thought about my son, and then I thought about God. Why was I being punished again? If my crime was a passion for helping others, it was time for me to end it all now. I looked around at the dozens of people happily walking past me, some finishing their workday, others with their hands full carrying Christmas presents home to their families.

I waited for the crowd to thin out, when, from out of nowhere a voice shouted my name, "Hey, Susan! I've been thinking about you. It's really great to see you! Do you have time to grab a cup of coffee?"

The man was a news reporter I'd known a few years.

"What's the matter?" John asked. I couldn't speak, I was crying uncontrollably and shivering in the cold. John held me in his arms as my tears turned into little icy droplets on his cashmere coat. He took a handkerchief from his pocket, placing it to my face.

"Come on, it's okay. Let's go across the street and get you a warm brandy."

"No, I'm fine really. Please, I have to be some place," I replied.

"Yes, with me! Come on, let's go," John said as he pulled me across the busy intersection and into the bar across the street. We sat at a quiet table away from the other patrons. John went up to the bar and returned with two large warm brandies.

"Here, drink up. It will make you feel better."

I didn't normally drink, but the warmth of the brandy felt soothing going down.

We sat in silence. I excused myself to go to the restroom. My face was flushed and my make-up had run down to my cheeks. At the sink, I put warm compresses on my face. I fixed myself up as best I could before going back into the bar.

"John ordered us two more. Susan what's wrong? Can I help you?"

I started to cry again, finally saying, "John, I just don't want to talk about it. There isn't anything anyone can do. I'll be alright. Really, I will."

We sat and made small talk for about an hour. When I left I walked back to my car in the parking garage. I flipped on my pager. Jennifer's office had called at least a dozen times. I stopped at a pay phone and called her.

"Where the hell are you?" Jennifer screamed into the phone.

I told her I had been walking around. Jennifer instructed me to stay at the parking garage, and she would be right over to meet me.

When she pulled up in her car she said, "You're coming with me to Michigan for the Christmas holidays."

"No, I'm not. I'll be fine," I said.

"Really? You call that outburst in court 'alright'? You look like shit and I don't believe it's in your best interest to be alone," she countered.

"Who said I was going to be alone? Jennifer, it's kind of you, but I'll take a rain check," I insisted.

"Sorry," Jennifer said, "but we're driving to your house. You'll pack a bag for a few days and we're driving to Michigan. I'm not taking 'no' for answer. You're in serious trouble with the court. I'm going to have to think about how to get you out of this mess. Susan, you can't yell and scream at a judge in a courtroom. They lock people up for what you did earlier today. I know you're upset and you have every right to be and we'll let it go for now, but eventually you'll have to apologize to the judge. Besides, you're a much better cook than I am, and we'll have fun. You'll see."

It took a day or so before my mood changed. Jennifer's extended family and friends came up to spend the holidays, and I stayed busy in the kitchen trying to keep my mind occupied on things other than my son.

Each morning I would take a cup of hot coffee and go for a long walk down to the beach. I stood on the snow banks, watching the water, thinking if God really existed he'd reveal a sign to me. Maybe an angel would stand next to me and whisper words of encouragement, or give me the answers to the hundreds of questions I had running through my mind. This helplessness was what I'd felt as kid.

Christmas morning was rough. While Jennifer's family sat around the tree opening presents I was in a corner watching the adults and kids fight over who would open what present. It was more then I could handle. Slowly I rose from the chair hoping no one would notice me leave the room.

"Hey Susan, where do you think you're going?" asked Jennifer. "Here, you can't go anywhere without opening your present."

My eyes swelled with tears as Jennifer handed me a huge box. It was a new printer for my computer. I thanked her.

We headed back to Chicago just before New Year's Eve, just in time for me to put on my party face and ring in the new year with some friends. I felt being around people was important. No one knew what had happened with my son. I'd kept silent trying to figure out how to deal with Vincent being gone and how to get him back.

With the new year came more women in need of services to escape their abusive and dangerous relationships. I immersed myself deeper into everyone else's life crises. I also had a status hearing on my son's case.

Before we began my lawyer took me into the judge's chambers to have me apologize for my outburst in court. The judge warned me if it happened again he would fine me $1,000 and ten days in jail.

In addition to everything else I also had a falling out with the security company providing protection for the victims. Sam, the owner of the security company, insisted I sign documents for contracts to do business with the city. I refused because I felt I was being railroaded into something involving my name and a large amount of money.

Sam came downtown to take me to dinner to discuss the matter. I had noticed, at other times during business meetings, that when he was lying about something, his nose twitched. That evening his pointy Italian nose might as well have fallen onto the table and danced!

"I understand you have some questions concerning the contracts we gave you to sign," he asked me.

I didn't care for Sam's tone of voice. It had a familiar sound, as if my father was ordering me to do something ... or else. Intuitively, I knew something wasn't right.

"No questions or concerns. I'm just not signing any contracts, nor will I be responsible for anything with that many zeros attached to it," I replied.

"Our company has provided hundreds of thousands of dollars in security to you and your clients. I expected in return you would do this small favor," he said to me.

"Sam, this isn't a favor. You're ordering me to sign my name to those contracts. Now you're attaching a price for the work that you referred to as 'giving back to society' when we first met," I replied.

Sam's face turned a deep shade of red. He stuck his neck out, tugging at his over starched shirt collar, he cleared his throat and said, "I'm trying to have a conversation with you like an adult. You're acting like a child. We need those contracts in order for our company to survive. Without revenue, we won't be able to provide security services to you in the future."

"Why are you so upset with me?" I asked him.

"Susan, I thought you understood. Someday I was going to ask you for a favor. That day is here." I was reminded of a scene from *The Godfather* where Marlon Brando's character says, "Someday, you will be called upon and expected to do a favor in return."

"Sam," I countered, "I'm not signing any documents or risking my name or reputation on contracts that don't benefit my organization and then lie about how the money's spent. Thank you for a lovely dinner. I'll see myself home."

Sam was snapping his fingers at me to return to the table at once. I didn't turn around. I hailed a cab and went home.

A few days later, I was served a law suit outside my office. Sam's company was suing me for breach of contract, for the sum of $1,999,999.

I called Jennifer and we discussed my latest bombshell.

"Susan, have you read through the lawsuit?"

"No," I replied.

Jennifer offered to read it aloud. I told her I didn't wish to hear it. My belief is that words, good or bad, have power in our lives. To read such a document would upset me and I'd internalize the fact someone was trying to hurt me. I'd already had enough of that on my plate.

What I wanted to know was who'd represent me to make it go away. She informed me it was not that easy and she needed to speak with someone experienced in contract law. In the lawsuit Sam claimed breach of contract and, like a hurt little boy, he was seeking damages in the same amount as the contracts I'd refused to sign.

"I'll find someone else to take the case," I said.

I scrambled to secure another security company to provide services to our clients. Once again, I moved into new offices.

As the court date for Sam's lawsuit got closer, I was unable to find a lawyer to represent me without a large retainer. One evening, at a political fund raiser, I ran into John Monroe, a handsome man in his late thirties, who'd followed in his father's political footsteps, quickly rising up the ranks as one of Mayor Daley's trusted advisors at the City of Chicago procurement office. We'd known each other for a few years, he was a staple at most political events.

John made small talk with me about what he'd known had happened with respect to my domestic violence agency. "Susan, have you ever heard the saying 'you'd get more with honey than vinegar?' I'm behind you one hundred percent, have been since day one. I get what you're doing. Your method is what's gotten you in a bind."

I didn't know how to respond. Casually, I mentioned the lawsuit from the security company against me. John's office approved city contracts for various services, including security. He was familiar with this particular company.

A few days later John called, asking if I could meet him for lunch.

At the restaurant, John proudly announced, in a tone as though he were my knight in shining armor, he'd arranged a meeting with "some influential people" to resolve my lawsuit with Sam and his company.

Later that day, John called asking me to meet him for a drink. "I'm meeting with Sam and a few, shall we say, influential business-men at a restaurant on the street corner of 17th and Taylor in about an hour. I thought you'd like to come along."

"No, I can't. Can you call me after the meeting," I asked.

The next morning, John called and we arranged to meet for coffee at a restaurant across from city hall.

"I wish you had been there. The look on Sam's face was priceless. When Sam saw who was seated in the room his mouth dropped open in shock," John told me.

I asked John to elaborate.

"Sam was summoned to a meeting with a group of powerful men of Italian heritage who had, shall we say, a way of helping people understand."

I interrupted, "The mafia? You'd arranged this with members of the mafia?"

"'Joey D' pulled out a shoe box and handed it to Sam. He ordered Sam to open it. 'Sam, do you see what is inside the box?' Susan, he was so scared he almost crapped in his pants."

"What was in the box?" I asked.

"Wait, I'm getting to the best part, next Joey said, 'If you don't drop the lawsuit against Susan, you're going to wind up like this dead mouse. *Capice?*'"

John continued, "Sam agreed, on one condition, I set up a meeting with you in my office. He wants to make it look like he has decided on his own to drop the lawsuit against you. Sam asked that you not be told how he arrived at his sudden change of heart."

This wasn't a secret. The City of Chicago and organized crime had been in bed together for many years. That's just how things operated behind the political scenes. The organized crime families would receive various service contacts for trash pick-up and supply materials for city streets and in return they'd repay the favor by working the precincts and making sure voters showed up at the polls. It was a hell of a racket.

Warmly, I hugged John and thanked him.

"How about you let me take you out to dinner and celebrate your victory?" I was flattered but I didn't feel it was a good idea. I didn't have the time nor energy for dating or relationships. I had an agency to run.

"Susan, you're very attractive and I've always wanted to go out with you."

I finally agreed to go out with him. But it felt awkward. Our relationship was more like brother and sister and I was all too familiar with his womanizing for any type of long term relationship.

I began drafting a book to help victims involved in abusive relationships. I used many of the cases I'd worked on as examples in creating my new book.

The State's Attorney was working on building a case against me, claiming I was practicing law without a license. I learned they had served subpoenas to a number of my domestic violence clients. Their goal was to indict me. Secretly a grand jury was held to determine if my services to victims constituted practicing law.

I'd arranged to meet with John to discuss my options.

"Why is the State's Attorney coming after me? I haven't done anything wrong except keep women from being murdered. Make it go away. I'm not going down for keeping these women alive, do you hear me," I explained.

"Look Susan, the State Attorney has an election coming up and he can't afford to have you continue to bash or embarrass him and his office in the media every time a case goes sour, or a woman is murdered. You have to admit that sometimes you take this cause to the extreme."

"Are you crazy, John? If his office did their damn jobs I wouldn't involve the media. Look what they did on the Connie Chaney case. Her husband held her hostage at gun point, raped her, and she barely escaped. Yet it takes them a few days to arrest him. Any idea what happened in court on this case? The Assistant State's Attorney misplaced Wayne Chaney's case file. Oh, wait and he's a Class X felon, too. No file, so the judge release's the piece of garbage on bond. If you're a Class X felon you automatically don't get bond. Days later Wayne Chaney murders Connie in a parking lot in Des Plaines. For ten days there is a manhunt until he is located and dies in a shoot out with sheriff's."

"Susan, that's what I meant, you just made my point. You went to the media toasting the State Attorney every day while Chaney was on the loose, publicly calling out his office and law enforcement for failing to do their jobs."

"John," I interrupted, "they didn't do their jobs!"

"Susan, stop interrupting me and let me finish. And you want to know why the State Attorney wants you out of the way? You're a political liability to his re-election."

"John, I'm so tired of this bullshit! I feel like a fighter in a boxing ring."

"Susan your Irish is showing, calm down."

"Don't tell me to calm down! You're telling me I have to play ball, but I don't have a choice. So it's their way or no way, right?"

John looked at me as if he were trying to find his words, clearing his throat, "Yes, your back is up against a wall. I see no other alternative for you but to accept their terms."

John's plan was to schedule a meeting with the Mayor and discuss a way that would benefit both the city and me. It was determined that if I agreed to remain silent for one year and didn't drop any bombshells in the media, assist a surviving family member, or file lawsuits then the city would see this as a sign of good faith and reciprocate by speaking to the State Attorney and having the Grand Jury quashed.

"Does that include my son's case, I asked? Can you arrange for me to see him?"

"No, I'm afraid I can't do anything with your custody case. That's a civil matter," said John.

Reluctantly, I agreed not to give media interviews or hold press conferences, or publicly pull down the pants of elected officials when they screwed up cases in court or cost victims of domestic violence their lives.

I worked on my book instead, *Defending Our Lives: Getting Away From Domestic Violence and Staying Safe.* After sending the finished manuscript to an agent I was invited to New York City to meet several senior editors from large book publishing houses.

After two days in New York, my agent explained the book was going to be put out for bid and sold at auction. Interested publishing houses would submit their offers in a sealed envelope for the rights to publish it. I was excited.

This was going to be a great way to reach out and assist victims and once the book was published my mother would forever be enshrined in the Library of Congress. In the silence of her death, she would finally be given an important voice in the battle to save others from the same fate.

Chapter Twelve
No Return

I was not looking forward to the meeting with the court appointed mental health evaluator after witnessing these professionals in court on other divorce cases. They were talented sharks swimming the waters with their hands open for payment as they assessed and determined the lives of total strangers.

After a full week of work at the domestic violence agency, I went to my first scheduled appointment. The psychologist's office was very basic and visually sterile. The walls were stark naked except for diplomas from a university out west. A cheap partition separated the room. "Hello! Come in," said a voice.

"Welcome. I'm Doctor Alan Chandler." As he walked over to me he commented, "My, my, you're very tall."

"It's the heels," I responded. "I'm Susan Milano."

"I know and I'm so excited! You're always on the news and I saw you on *Oprah* discussing the topic of domestic violence a few weeks ago."

The doctor explained I would be taking a written psychological test and we would meet for a session at the end of the following week.

"I won't be here when you finish. I have a pedicure appointment. You can let yourself out after you have completed the test." He said goodbye and I sat at a desk reviewing the test which consisted of multiple choice psychological questions. Seventy-five percent of the questions had nothing to do with parenting. It took two hours to complete. I left and met some friends for dinner.

My book agent from New York City called with good news—Doubleday Publishing had purchased the rights to my book.

"What does that mean?" I asked.

"Well, it means you're under contract with them. Any rewrites or changes to your manuscript have to be completed by an agreed upon deadline. In summary, within the year your book will be published. Congratulations!"

I called around to my friends, announcing the news. In my office, I twirled in my chair like a child. That evening, just as I was leaving the office, I received a call from a client who said the battered women's shelters were full and she had no place to stay for the night. I was concerned for her because she was due in court in the morning on an order of protection hearing.

"Kim, where are you?" I asked.

"I'm not far from your office," she replied.

I asked her to walk over and I called around to women's shelters. Staying at a shelter for battered women would keep her in a safe environment away from further harm. However, they were all full, just like she'd said.

A restaurant convention was in town and the hotels didn't have any vacancies either. When Kim arrived at my office, we walked to my car at the parking garage. She needed to make a stop and pick up her son from day care. Kim was an attractive, 34-year-old redhead, mother of a five-year-old boy named Matthew. She worked as a secretary for a major accounting firm. Her husband, a pharmacist, was controlling and violent. He had threatened to kill her if she ever left him. A week before neighbors had called the police because they'd heard Kim pleading for her life while her husband beat her.

Police had arrested the husband and he remained in jail for 24 hours, just enough time for Kim to pack what she needed to get away. She'd completed a police report and would be going to court for a criminal order of protection.

In the car, Kim apologized, "I'm so sorry to be such a burden and cause you all this trouble."

I responded that she wasn't a burden. "The shelters and hotels are full. Once we pick up your son you're coming with me for the night and then we'll go to court in the morning."

Kim felt bad and didn't want to impose. Frankly, I was happy for the company. Most evenings I went home to an empty house. I was unable to see or even speak to my son over the telephone. His father was manipulative. He would either hang up on me when I asked to speak with Vincent or not answer the phone.

Bringing someone to my home was rare, but this was an emergency. We picked up her son and a pizza on the way. Once inside, her little boy took off his coat and asked for something to drink.

My son's room was filled with toys. When I brought Matthew into Vincent's bedroom his blue eyes widened, "Oh, wow! Whose is all this?" he asked.

"I arranged it special, just for you. Why don't we eat some pizza and then you can come in and play with the toys."

My son's room was decorated in his favorite Power Ranger theme, with sheets, curtains, and posters on the walls. When it was time for Kim to put Matthew to bed, I heard her son say a prayer, "Thank you Jesus, for keeping my mommy and me safe and for all the cool toys."

Kim returned to the living room and we sat and had coffee. I pointed to the bathroom. "There's everything you need, just help yourself. There are some tooth brushes in the medicine cabinet and below the sink are some other toiletries."

"I can't thank you enough. This is above and beyond," said Kim.

"Please," I replied, "I'm happy to do it. You can stay here until we have things figured out."

The following morning, after dropping off Matthew, Kim and I went to court. She was granted a temporary order of protection by a judge and was scheduled to return in twenty-one days. Kim and her son remained with me for the three weeks, until she was able to rent an apartment in the city. We worked on a safety plan for the two of them. Her husband attempted to communicate with her by sending flowers with notes of affection, asking for Kim and her son to return.

His notes would read, "Please my darling, give me, give us, give our family another chance. I'm sorry for hurting you. I will never lay a hand on you again, you have my word."

The notes and flowers were a direct violation of Kim's court order of protection which prohibited all forms of communication as stated in the judge's court order. Kim returned back to court to stop the harassing calls at work, the letters, notes, and gifts.

I was not looking forward to my return visit with the psychologist. I noticed during my next visit he seemed taller. Looking down at his shoes I noticed he was wearing lifts to make him appear taller. I tried not to laugh.

"Before we begin, can we discuss another matter?" he asked, "I was wondering if you'd consider consulting me on possible opportunities with the media. Of course, I'd pay you..."

After he finished with his idea, he asked what I thought of his proposal. I didn't know how to respond. I wanted to ask what any of this had to do with seeing my son. My life, and that of Vincent's was in this bozo's hands! One wrong response could cost me the chance to see my son again.

"Well, sure, I'd be happy to provide direction with media appearances," I replied.

"Great," replied the doctor. "It was my significant other's idea. I told him you were in my office, his name is Peter. We've been together for six years and he was so excited I would be talking to you. He's looking forward to meeting you too. We'd love to have you over for dinner. Peter is an excellent cook. There I go rambling again. Anyway, thank you," replied the doctor.

We didn't talk about how much longer this process would take before I could see my son. Our conversation was mostly about the doctor and his personal life. Like when he first knew he was gay, and how his parents took the news of his gay lifestyle choice. "This can't be happening," I thought to myself.

When I spoke with Jennifer about my sessions, she thought I should go to the professional licensing board and file a formal complaint against Dr. Chandler. "Unfortunately," I declared, "the last thing I needed to do was file a complaint against the man who held all the power in deciding Vincent's life."

My literary Agent called to update me on the progress of my book. "We're right on schedule. I'm pleased with the changes you made too. It looks like your book will be released in October, right in time for National Domestic Violence Awareness month."

My book editor instructed me to have a professional photo taken for inside the book jacket and to plan to be in New York City in the spring to meet with various editorial staff for book reviews and a pre-press launch.

A police detective called me to say that Kim was in the police station asking to speak with me. "Hi, Susan," her voice sounded very nervous and shaky, "my husband followed me to the day care center and when I got out of my car to pick-up Matthew he grabbed me from behind, slamming me down onto the pavement. Then he started kicking me, demanding to know where I've been living. I'm here at the police station filling out a report and talking to the detective."

"Kim, are you alright?" I asked.

She was badly shaken, but it was nothing serious. I spoke with the detective and asked him to contact the State's Attorney office to see if they could file stalking and battery charges against Kim's husband. He was going to check and get back with me. My concern was that Kim's husband was still out there someplace and I wasn't sure what he'd do next.

I gave the detective my address and asked that she follow Kim and her son to my house. Under the circumstances I didn't want Kim to return to her own apartment, especially at night.

I greeted Kim and her son at the front door. "Hi, Miss Susan," her son said. Matthew offered his hand to give me a high five.

"My mommy and I decided to have a sleep over at your house again."

"That's wonderful. You and your mom are welcome anytime," I told him.

While Matthew played in the bedroom, I said, "Kim, I think we need to change where your son goes to day care. It's not safe anymore. I've made arrangements with a woman I know to watch your son until you find a new day care center. She'll be here in about an hour to meet you. If you like her, Matthew can go there in the morning. She's a retired sheriff's deputy and has a grandchild about your son's age she watches too." Kim agreed to meet her and the two women hit it off. Kim was very comfortable with the temporary arrangement for her son.

I prepared an affidavit for the day care center with instructions for them to follow if Kim's husband were to show up. I also provided them a current photo, year, make, and model of his vehicle. Knowing what to do and how to handle the situation if Kim's husband called or showed up was important.

The next few weeks were hectic. I was on deadline with revisions for my book and had yet another appointment with the psychologist. Our next session would be at my home, with the doctor and my son. The object was for the doctor to observe how I interacted with Vincent. I was nervous. It had been over a year-and-a-half since my son and I were together. I prepared all of my son's favorite foods—a fresh turkey with all the trimmings and strawberry ice cream for desert.

Vincent's father brought him into the house. The doctor was already there waiting when they arrived. At first Vincent was hesitant, clinging to his father. I approached my son with caution.

"Mommy is so happy to see you. Is it okay if I give you a hug?"

Once in my arms Vincent cried, "I missed you, Mommy."

"Shush, it's okay, I missed you too. Are you hungry?" I asked.

"Uh huh," responded Vincent.

"I made your favorite meal."

"Oh, turkey! Mommy, you made me turkey!"

I had to smile when I'd wanted to cry. How long I hugged my own son was being monitored by a stop watch.

"Yes baby, how about we sit at the table and eat?" The doctor greeted my son. I didn't know they'd already met.

Vincent's father decided to invite himself by grabbing a plate and sitting down to eat. I didn't want him here. I shot the doctor a disapproving look, but the message didn't get through.

"Vincent, how about your Dad stays and eats with us and then comes back later to pick you up?" asked the doctor.

Vincent was too busy gazing at the food on the table to pay much attention.

Sadly, from the looks of my son, he had gained at least 20 pounds. It was obvious he'd been fed a steady diet of junk food, something I never allowed him to eat.

When it was time for Vincent's father to leave, his father asked, "Vincent, are you sure you feel safe here?"

I did all I could to bite the inside of my cheek not to respond. His father was playing a dangerous game with my child.

"Vincent, Daddy won't be far. If you get scared call me, I'll come and get you."

"Is that really necessary?" I asked.

"Yes, Susan it is. Vincent and I openly discussed his fear of seeing you again," said his father.

"Fear? You put that in his head! You've brainwashed our own son."

The doctor interrupted, "Dad, I think we'll be fine."

It was awkward having the doctor monitor my interactions with my own son. Two hours later, Vincent's father returned to take him back and continued with his tactics.

"Everything go okay, doc?" he asked.

I wanted to scream. As if I would ever do anything to hurt or harm my own son.

When my son and his father left, the doctor and I spoke briefly. The doctor indicated he was happy with the interaction between me and Vincent.

I was livid. The entire afternoon was a farce so the doctor could document interaction for the court record. I'd seen this song through the years play out in many cases when a victim ended her relationship with a psychopath. I knew the sheet music by heart. The decision for custody and visitation had already been made. Worst of all I had one more mandatory session to endure.

Kim's situation escalated. Her husband tried to abduct her from the parking lot where she worked.

By the time police arrived, Kim's husband had fled. Witnesses provided details of the failed abduction. I contacted the State's Attorney office requesting charges be increased to felony stalking.

Kim had some vacation time coming and I suggested she take it. Until her husband was arrested she wasn't safe to return to work.

I placed a security detail with Kim and her son. A few days later, a detective called to say Kim's husband had been arrested. Kim had a divorce hearing the next day.

Her husband was brought in by the bailiff wearing a Cook County orange jumpsuit and leg shackles. The judge raised his brow, looking at Kim's husband, before he spoke. Then the judge requested the criminal case file from the State's Attorney's office.

Unable to post the high bond of $100,000, Kim's husband would remain behind bars until his criminal trial for stalking and other related charges occurred.

Kim's divorce attorney was able to ask for sole custody and remove visitation with ease. The judge also granted Kim the ability to move out of state. It was a victory. Kim's husband was eventually sentenced to five years in prison for attempted murder, stalking, and a weapons charge for a gun the police found when they arrested him. Kim eventually moved out of state.

At the last minute, Dr. Chandler called and instructed me to meet him for lunch at a restaurant up the street from his office. When I arrived, I found the doctor seated at a table where everyone would notice him. I said hello and asked the restaurant manager to move us to a table in the back. I was disgusted with the doctor. It was obvious he regularly ate at this establishment and was familiar with the staff and patrons.

The entire time, the doctor rudely waved people over to our table. "You see who I'm having lunch with?" he announced.

I wanted to hide under the table, but it wasn't large enough for me to fit. Restaurant patrons continued to walk up and shake my hand. When I attempted to discuss the report he would be turning into the court on visitation and custody of my child, the doctor quickly changed the conversation.

During the next court date, the doctor submitted his report to the court pertaining to visitation. The report was not favorable. I was only given one day a week to see my son, and no overnight visitation. I was devastated. There was no chance of ever regaining custody or having a healthy relationship with my son.

Jeff took every opportunity to shoot me his infamous "gotcha" smile in court. He'd won, taking away the only person whom mattered in my life: my son. This wasn't a victory. Vincent's life would be forever altered. I'd seen the effects on other children whose mothers were ripped out from their lives. These children grew up to be angry, dangerous, and resentful adults, unable to have healthy loving relationships of their own.

On this day in court, my son lost his mother and I lost my son. He would never know me as anything more than a visitor in his life.

Chapter Thirteen
Making the World a Better Place

The release of my new book was just weeks away. Doubleday books scheduled me for a major ten-city book tour during the month of October. I made arrangements with interns and Jennifer to cover the client case load while I was gone. In anticipation of the games my son's father would play, I sent a certified letter to both he and my lawyer indicating I wouldn't exercise my visitations for the month of October, resuming my visits at the start of November. I sent the letter certified with a signature request, just in case my son's father decided to say I was not following the court visitation agreement. Two weeks before I was scheduled to leave my son's father decided to play his games again.

On Sunday morning, as I drove to pick up my son to go fishing and a picnic, I pulled over, calling from the road to give my estimated time of arrival. No one answered the phone.

I was concerned but went to my son's house anyway. I parked in front of the house and rang the doorbell, no one answered. Their car was not parked in front. I called my former mother in-law thinking she might be home, "Hi Peg, is Vincent there?" I asked.

"No," she replied. And before I could ask her if she knew where he could be, she'd hung up.

I waited on the stoop for about three hours. I continued to call his father's phone but he didn't pick up. I left and headed home. The drive back was about two hours. Sunday traffic was brutal because of a White Sox's game and a concert in the city. A few minutes after I got home I checked my messages on the answering machine. Vincent's father had called several times, "Susan where are you? Vincent is waiting to go fishing." The time indicated on the answering machine showed he had pretended to be calling from his house while waiting for me.

This was the type of reoccurring and cruel game he played. From my home computer I e-mailed my attorney with the exact times and messages left on the machine as well as letting him know when my toll-way receipt number had been stamped and dated. A week before I was scheduled to leave, and the last scheduled Sunday visitation until November with my son, his father played the same cat and mouse game.

The initial week of the tour I was scheduled to be in San Francisco and Los Angeles. I realized this was the first time since my parent's deaths I had been away. Being able to travel, and knowing my agency was in good hands, was a relief.

I felt like I had a magical fairy angel with me on my book tour. The accommodations were first class. In each city I was assigned an escort. Their duties included picking me up at the airport, taking me to my hotel, calling ahead, and making sure everything was ready for my speaking engagements and book signings. If I accidently snagged my panty hose, without missing a beat, my escort asked me what size I wore and in the blink of an eye, the problem was solved and we were on our way to the next event. I learned there were also male escorts, but most of the time they were women: mothers and retirees that knew each city, loved to read, and most of all meet new people. They would be with me from the time of my first appointment until the very last engagement, including any television and radio appearances. Sometimes the days would last until midnight.

After the west coast, I was sent to Detroit and then Atlanta. On the plane from Detroit to Atlanta I struck up a conversation with a senior executive with *Essence* magazine who was on his way to interview the well-known lawyer Johnny Cochran and Planned Parenthood's Faye Wattleton. Both of them had just authored new books.

"I'm a newly published author too," I declared and proudly took out a copy of my book to give him.

He extended his hand and introduced himself. "This really looks interesting, congratulations," he said as he handed back the book.

I pushed it back. "No, no, keep it, maybe your magazine can do a story or excerpt on the book."

"We're an African American publication," he said. "We only feature African Americans in the magazine."

I thought for a moment then I pulled the safety pin I always carried in my bra out. With a look of surprise, the man backed into his seat.

"Wait, if I prick my finger I'll draw blood. Is there any difference between the color of my blood and your blood?" I asked.

"No, there's not," he responded.

I continued, "The information in this book is important for anyone in any abusive relationship. Domestic abuse and murder isn't race specific. So why would a magazine be color blind to information that saves lives?" I asked.

"Point taken," he replied.

I went further and talked about my own personal tragedy. I'd forgotten about my encounter on the plane until my book agent called.

"Susan, I just had the strangest conversation with someone from *Essence* magazine. Whatever you said left a lasting impression. They're going to publish excerpts from your book in February. Susan, I have to ask you, do you always whip out safety pins and prick your finger?" she asked.

"I was just trying to make a point. It worked, that's all that matters," I added.

Before I left a city I would always stop and buy something for Vincent. I tried to call and speak with him while I was away but his father never answered the phone. On my trip to Boston we had difficulty at the airport and I didn't arrive until 3 AM. I was tired and couldn't wait to lay my head on a pillow. As I was checking into the hotel, the clerk informed me I'd be staying in the author's suite. "Why was he telling me that," I thought to myself. There were several faxes and messages when I arrived as well.

One was from my Editor at Doubleday. The message read, "Enjoy, Susan, this is my gift to you." I opened the door to a most breath taking room. The bellman explained that author's such as Truman Capote and Gore Vidal, among other literary giants, had stayed in this very suite.

The décor was dark walnut, set with grace and elegance. Double French doors opened to a master bedroom large enough for Abraham Lincoln. Carefully arranged in a locked glass bookcase were books personally signed by the authors who'd stayed in the suite. Another set of French doors took you out to the balcony overlooking the river. It was truly magical. On the coffee table was an oversized book with a note asking that the author occupying the suite leave their words of wisdom and sign their name. I sat in a large oversized chair, reading thought provoking words of wisdom written by fellow authors. I read till the wee hours of the morning.

I dozed off in the chair and missed my wake-up call. A bellman arrived at my door with a note that read, "Lucky was in the hotel driveway waiting for me in a black Lexus."

I gathered my thoughts, jumped in the shower and got ready in record time. I was in deep fog. I ran out of the hotel and into a black Lexus parked out in front where a handsome man, in his early forties, waited for me at the wheel.

I rambled, "I'm so sorry to be so late but there was this amazing book with notes from other authors and I stayed up to read as many pages as possible..."

"Where are we going," he asked with a big cat-like smile on his face.

Next, I heard a tap on my window from the bellman, "Miss, you're in the wrong car, your party is across the island waiting for you."

"Oh my God, I'm so embarrassed," I tried to talk but without my wake-up cup of morning java I was tongue tied.

"No problem ma'am, my name is Ben and the pleasure, I assure you, is all mine."

"I really should be going," I replied.

"I'd love to see you again," he said, then asked, "How long are you in town?"

Words would not come out of my mouth. "Um, well, I have to go."

When I finally got in the right car, Lucky, my escort, who was a woman, and I laughed the entire morning about my mistake. Strangley, they each drove a black Lexus and I'd just assumed Lucky was a man's name.

My escort dropped me off at the hotel for a mid-afternoon nap. "I'll return at 4 PM sharp, try not to run into the wrong car this time," she laughed.

I stopped at the hotel desk to pick up my messages on the way to my room. There was handwritten note in an envelope addressed to me: "Susan, please have dinner with me this evening." The note was signed by Ben, with his mobile number included.

I opened the door to my suite and the place looked like a flower shop. There were several dozen roses, in red, pink, and yellow. Each with a funny note attached. "You have to meet me for dinner, my heart cannot deal with rejection." Another note read, "I know as you're reading these words your head is saying no, but ah, the heart is saying yes."

I checked my itinerary, called Ben, and arranged to meet him the following night at the hotel for dinner.

The following day was hectic. I had five live, in-studio radio interviews and two television shows to do, all before noon.

I walked into the first radio studio surprised to see Ben at the microphone. The producer let me into the radio booth at the next station break.

I smiled from ear to ear as I sat across Ben. It was difficult to discuss the book while he continued to smile and wink at me.

When the interview ended, Ben grabbed my arm, "I'll see you later."

"You aren't going to meet him are you?" asked my motherly Jewish escort.

"I most certainly am." I answered.

"Susan, do you realize he owns the radio station and other media in town?"

The producer in the sound room claimed he'd never seen his boss take over the morning show and conduct an interview. Then he added, "I watched the heated exchange between the two of you. I hope you know what you're doing."

That evening Ben and I met in the hotel bar. After we finished our drink, Ben insisted we leave the bar and get into the limo that was waiting in front of the hotel. He wore black ostrich cowboy boots, jeans, and a blue, button down shirt that matched his eyes. His cologne was rugged yet not overpowering.

Ben owned several commercial buildings located in the heart of the city's financial district. We had dinner on a rooftop. A table was beautifully set and a string quartet played. A bottle of bubbly was chilling on the table. I don't know where the time went. We never made it to desert. Ben grabbed me in a lip lock and when I looked at the time it was past two in the morning. "I really have to be going, thank you for a splendid evening," I said.

On the way back to my hotel Ben asked if we could see other for breakfast. I agreed since I probably wasn't going to get much sleep.

Breakfast and Ben arrived at the same time. We sat in the living room of my suite, barely touching our food because we were so busy talking. "Can I come to Chicago?" asked Ben, "or better yet I'll send a plane for you and we can go to Martha's Vineyard for a long weekend?"

My response was I'd have to check my schedule. While he was using the bathroom, I noticed his wallet on the table and decided to copy his personal information. I didn't care who he was, I still had to check him out. Before I got on the plane back to Chicago I called a private eye to obtain a full history on him.

When I returned home I called my son. There was no answer but I left him a message just the same. Sadly, I always assumed he was never told when I called, or about any messages I left for him.

I had exactly 24 hours before I headed to Washington, DC. Ben called to say hello, asking if I'd arrived safely. He couldn't wait to see me. We stayed on the phone, but I cut our conversation short to run some errands. Ben called again to wish me good night, but I was out having dinner with friends.

The following day I got on a plane for Washington. The information on Ben arrived the next day. My suspicions were correct. Ben was married and had four children. Something he forgot to mention. I wrote down all the details. I purposely avoided Ben's calls until returning back home.

There were several panicky messages from Ben asking why I hadn't called him back. I sat on the couch, took a deep breath and dialed the telephone number given to me by the person who ran a background check for me.

I blocked out my number when I called. Ben answered. He heard my voice and froze. In a whisper he said he would call me back in 20 minutes, but I didn't need an explanation of the obvious. I never spoke with him again.

I finished the book tour and resumed my schedule. The holidays were approaching and I asked my lawyer to file a motion with the court asking for three or four days during Christmas holidays with my son.

I got a lucky break, the regular judge was out due to illness for several weeks and a new judge was presiding over the court cases.

We stood before the temporary judge as she read the file, looking up every so often she shifting her eyes between both lawyers. "I need more time to study the file," she announced, setting a continuance for the following week. I was elated. I was hopeful the custody case would turn around and I'd be able to be with Vincent.

When we returned the following week the judge took a deep breath and looked at all of us before speaking. "I don't know how a mother can be ripped from her son with nothing more than allegations thrown against a wall," she began.

My son's father tried to speak, "Mr. Milano do not interrupt me. Today, I will rule on visitation during the holidays and set another date after the new year for the court to reevaluate what's transpired."

Jeff continued to interrupt, only to fuel the judge, "Counsel, I will not tolerate your clients outbursts in my courtroom!"

Amidst furious objections from Jeff's attorney, I was granted four days and three overnights through Christmas Eve at 6 PM. The judge informed Jeff that if he didn't comply with the court order, he'd be in contempt and arrested.

Before the judge concluded she added, "Mr. Milano, I know what you're up too, and sir, I can see right through you."

I was so thankful. Finally someone could see the lies orchestrated in the custody case. By the grace of God my prayers were answered.

We left the courtroom and my lawyer filed paperwork to have my custody case moved onto the new judge's court case calendar. I was elated. This was the first positive movement since Vincent was taken away from me. I went Christmas shopping and planned to make all Vincent's favorite foods.

Shortly after this good news I was summoned to a meeting at the Mayor's office. My agreement to play ball and be silent had ended. City officials wanted to create a women's office on domestic violence through their offices and they wanted my input. Although it was never discussed, I think the release of my book had something to do with their decision. I was happy to see the creation of this new division, but I made it clear I wanted no part of the carrot they were dangling in front of me to participate as an employee.

Their plan became crystal clear when we discussed the upcoming law suit filed against the police department and the City of Chicago involving Brenda Jordan. Brenda was shot moving items from her home while trying to leave her abusive husband of over ten years.

Brenda Jordan had secured a court order of protection that included authorizing a police presence for her while retrieving her personal items and documents. According to witness accounts, the police went up to the door of the residence. When the husband answered one of the officers asked if, "he was going to be a good boy while Brenda got some things she needed from the house."

"Oh yes, sir, she can come right on in," the husband had replied.

The responding officers didn't think it was important enough to ask the husband to step outside until his wife finished. Instead the police officers laughed and joked, drank coffee, and smoked cigarettes beside their squad cars.

Within ten minutes shots were fired with a semi-automatic weapon inside the house. The officers ducked for cover and Brenda lay lifeless in between the front door and the first step of her home, thirty-seven shots to her body. The police shouted for the husband to drop his weapon, but he continued firing more rounds at the officers before finally taking his own life.

When relatives from Brenda's family had contacted me two years earlier, I'd met with them and secured a lawyer to represent the family in a wrongful death suit. The trial date was now days away and city officials inquired as to my continued involvement. I didn't respond. My pager went off and I used it as an excuse to step out and thus, end the meeting.

Two days before the trial, the family, the supporters, the attorney, and I held a press conference. Our focus was to move forward with the case. We'd been working on the case nearly two years. The City of Chicago continued to ask a judge for new trial dates in hopes of wearing down the family. The day before the trial the attorney for the family received a call to meet with the city's attorney to discuss an out-of-court settlement. The lawyer called and gave me a synopsis of the meeting.

He said the City of Chicago would settle under the condition that I was not part of the discussion and agreed not to have any further discussions with the media about the case. I agreed.

The family won a monetary settlement of over a million dollars.

I cleared my calendar to prepare for Vincent. I bought a nine-foot Christmas tree and dragged it up the steps into the house. I went in the storage unit and unpacked the Christmas ornaments my mother had saved from our holidays.

Cheerfully, with Bing Crosby in the background singing corny holiday music, I decorated the tree and wrapped presents. When I went to pick up my son, but I decided not to take any chances and brought a girlfriend and her two children along for the ride as witnesses in case no one was home. We even took a video camera in case Vincent's father decided to pull a stunt. When I pulled up to the house, Vincent's father peered out the living room window. When he opened the door, he held his hand out for me to wait outside. He asked who was in the car. I responded loud enough for Vincent to hear that there were two other kids he was familiar with and their mother.

Without incident Vincent, now seven years old, carried his packman, I took his duffel bag, and we left. We all had dinner together. My girlfriend and her kids left. Vincent asked to make Christmas cookies for Santa, "Oh, and Mommy, we have to test them before we put them out for Santa Claus."

I laughed. I lifted him up onto the counter and he selected the decorations to put on top of the cookies. I made a triple batch of cookie dough. We put our first cookie sheet in and both sat on the floor next to the oven. I remembered my son had not seen my book. I excused myself and returned back to the floor.

"Do you know Mommy wrote a book?"

"Kinda" he replied.

We never really talked about what I did and why I helped people. I thought that discussion should happen when he got older. I opened the book to the acknowledgement page and ran my index finger along each word as I read it aloud:

"And finally, to my precious gift of love and joy, my child. It is for you that I have written this book. It is my hope that someday you understand that I wanted the world to be a better place."

"Mommy, where's my name?" he asked.

I replied, "You're my only child. I wrote this especially just for you. I love you and have missed you so much."

Vincent jumped into my lap, wrapped his arms tightly around my neck and cried, "Mommy, me too, I missed you so much."

We both cried for about ten minutes. Smoke started to fill the kitchen, we'd burned our first batch of cookies. We laughed and finished our baking.

Vincent asked if I could read him a story in the big bed in my bedroom. Of course I would. We both fell asleep. When I woke up in the morning Vincent was sleeping peacefully, still cradled underneath my arm.

Chapter Fourteen
Honey and Biscuits

Kicking in the new year with the hope I'd finally be able to spend more time with my son made everything around me feel and look brighter. Demands on my schedule increased with invitations for speaking engagements and a heavier volume of calls providing services to victims.

Over the weekend as I was cleaning out the closets I dragged out a large box labeled: "DANGER DO NOT OPEN." I carefully moved the taped cardboard box as though it contained explosives. Inside were the tapes and journals from my father. I became sick to my stomach as one-by-one I emptied the contents. I'd finally decided that keeping his tapes and journals along with other items served no purpose. The following day I took the box away and had it destroyed.

The first day of the new year at the office was hectic. Among the messages on the voice mail was a well-known, pricey divorce lawyer who'd left a message to make contact with him regardless of the hour. Although nearly ten in the evening I placed a call to his office. He answered, surprised, "Jerry, its Susan, I'm returning your call. Should we schedule a time to talk tomorrow?"

"No my dear," the elderly lawyer's voice chuckled. He'd met with a woman seeking a lawyer to represent her on an appeal in a custody case. She'd spent nearly $100,000 to settle her divorce case.

He continued, "The ex-father-in-law, a well known litigator, has seen to it that his former daughter-in-law has both mentally and financially exhausted all her resources. I feel you're the best person to secure this woman quality pro-bono representation in this matter."

I took down the woman's information and told Jerry I'd contact her within the week.

For my birthday a group of close friends had a birthday party for me at Russo's on Rush Street in Chicago. We were having a fantastic time.

I excused myself and went to the ladies room. Walking back to the table I was grabbed from behind, "Happy Birthday!"

I twisted my body to see who it was, "Oh my God, David, what are you doing here?"

"I was sitting at the bar having a drink when I caught you out of the corner of my eye walking past me."

I introduced David to everyone at the table. Jennifer invited him to sit down with us and have a drink. Jennifer noticed how cozy we were catching up on old times. Through the year's time had been good to David, he'd retained his youthful appearance.

"So, David, how do you know Susan?" Jennifer asked.

That same boyish smile I remembered appeared on David's face as he answered. He looked at me, "God, what's it been 20 years?"

We had known each other in high school. He continued talking, "I think the last time we were together was up at a quarry during a huge party the week before everyone headed off to college."

Jennifer asked what he did for a living. "I own a large medical supply company."

Jennifer continued, running her mouth like a mother hen asking questions.

"Alright counselor, that's enough for now," I finally said.

In between conversations, with everyone else at the table, David and I managed to catch up. "I have a boy, 13, and a girl, 10," said David. It's funny to run into you now. "Patty and I aren't married any more. Matter of fact our divorce was final exactly ten days ago."

"Oh, the ink's still wet." I replied.

David pulled his chair closer to me, we continued talking and whispering into each other's necks. I looked into his golden green eyes, yep, he could eat crackers in my bed anytime. David stayed and had dinner with us. When the waitress came over to put down the check, David immediately grabbed it and handed her a credit card, "I've got it."

Amidst protest from others at the table, David said, "please, it's my honor."

Jennifer shot me a look of approval that said she liked this man. As everyone began to leave David suggested the two of us go someplace for a cocktail.

The way David said cocktail made me giggle like a school girl. My mind was definitely elsewhere. David and I were discussing my work. At some point during the conversation he made a half-baked comment, "I know all too well what happens when police respond to a domestic violence call."

His comment immediately sent a red flag up in my mind. "Really David, how do you know so much?" I asked.

He casually mentioned his experience as if he were having a tooth extracted at the dentist. "Patty and I had a heated argument. She wanted me out of the house. Next thing I knew Patty smacked me on the side of the head with a frying pan. I reacted by hitting her and broke her nose. She called the police who walked in and saw Patty's face. They didn't ask my side of things and took me to jail in handcuffs."

"What happened next?" I asked.

"Oh nothing," said David, "the whole thing was eventually dropped." David's account of the events didn't sound accurate to me.

I excused myself, went into the ladies room where there was a pay phone, called the suburban police department and asked for a favor, "Hey, can you run a check on someone for me?"

The detective said the name sounded familiar, but he couldn't check for me right away because the system was down. I asked the detective to call me back as soon as possible.

We drove to the lake and stayed on the beach long enough to find ourselves watching the sunrise in between heavy lip locking action. When he finally took me home we made plans to meet for brunch and spend the day together. I took a nap and got ready to meet David downtown.

After brunch we walked to Navy Pier. While we were on the ferris wheel my pager went off, I looked down and it was the suburban police department calling me back.

"Here," said David, "use my phone."

"No, I'll wait until the ride ends." After speaking to the detective, I was disappointed. I thanked him and walked around the pier with David thinking of how to broach the subject. I finally brought up the subject.

"You know and understand what I do for a living, right?"

David replied, "Yes."

"Then why didn't you tell me you were charged with domestic battery?" I asked.

"Wait. What? Who told you that?" he asked.

"A birdie," I responded.

David's face turned beat red with anger. "I already told you what happened, end of story!"

"No David, you left out the part where you'd plead no contest and received six months probation. In my book, that's serious."

"How did you find out that information? The entire incident should have been expunged from my record!"

"Never mind," I replied, "You also left out the fact that you plead no contest, not once, but twice. And police responded to calls at your home address on several occasions."

"Susan, what the hell!? Okay I made a mistake, why keep talking about it like I committed an armed robbery. I was defending myself," David said.

I immediately replied, "I stand for the safety of women's lives. If I continue seeing you that makes me a hypocrite. David, do you even understand? Domestic violence is a serious crime. That's why you were arrested and charged."

David was not getting my point. He continued arguing with me saying, "I'm not an angry person, nor am I violent, now come on you're totally over reacting."

No matter what I did or didn't feel about the situation, once I learned the truth, seeing David on a personal level was not going to happen. I said goodbye and walked to my car.

David continued to call and leave messages for several weeks asking me to reconsider my decision. I never responded. It was back to calls and cases for me.

When I'd first reached Kathryn, the woman seeking a pro bono attorney for her custody case, she, as with most people I speak to during an initial conversation, talked a mile a minute.

I finally had to interrupt her. "Kathryn, please," I asked, "I need to ask you some questions," but she continued to go into great detail about her abusive marriage and subsequent divorce.

"Alright, please stop," I interrupted, "you need to give me yes or no answers without all the details or I'm not going to be able to help you."

Kathryn had been in divorce court for three years and had every single court appearance and filing on her case in eight large banker's boxes. I explained what I needed from her in order to call around town to secure an attorney. Kathryn insisted we meet in person. She wanted to personally bring all the journals and case files she'd maintained.

"No," I explained, "what I need, in less than twenty typed pages, is a summary of your case. I need the final decree and visitation agreement. Then you will drop it off in an envelope with my name on it at the law offices of Jennifer Waters on LaSalle Street and call me."

"Why? Why can't we meet in person?" Kathryn demanded.

"It's safer this way, you have to trust me," I explained. "And my time is very limited." Finally, she agreed to do as I asked.

Over the weekend Jeff called to say Vincent was too sick for me to take him on Sunday. But when I called to see what was actually wrong there was no answer. I e-mailed my attorney with the date and time of the message left on my answering machine. Jeff continued with these tactics for the next month. We went back into court to petition for visitation.

At the next court hearing, in response to my motion for a new judge and parental interference, Vincent's father walked into the courtroom half hunched over with a cane as if he were playing hurt. I could smell he was up to something.

As I tried to approach him, he shouted in the courtroom, "get her away from me." He'd concocted a new scheme to continue keeping my son away from me. He now claimed that during a scheduled visitation I'd hit and pushed him so hard that the fall had caused him a back injury. His accusations were crazy. I hadn't been able to reach anyone by phone whenever I called to schedule a pick-up time for Vincent. Thank goodness I'd kept my attorney informed and documented everything.

Although I'd been denied access to my son for weeks, Jeff continued his charade. Our case was called and we went up before the judge who addressed the motion for a new judge. He declared, "Counselor the case stays here, your motion is denied."

Jeff blurted out, "Your honor my lawyer couldn't be here today and I've meet with the State's Attorney to obtain a criminal order of protection, for the safety of my son and me. My injuries were caused by Susan. For the sake of my son's safety, I cancelled visitation."

My attorney responded, "Your honor, Mr. Milano is obviously lying, my client has repeatedly been denied access to her son." The judge looked at me, then looked over at Vincent's father before responding. "Mr. Milano do you have a police report on the alleged incident and order of protection?"

"Your Honor, I'm meeting with the State's Attorney immediately following this hearing." The judge raised his brow in disbelief, "We are going to take a 30-minute recess" said the judge.

The judge returned to the bench, saying he'd contacted the State's Attorney.

"Mr. Milano are you aware that I can have the sheriff lock you up immediately for lying to the court? The State's Attorney's office indicates they have no record of a conversation with you and there is no pending matter for an order of protection." Politely the Judge continued to speak about the importance of a healthy relationship between both parents.

The judge then scheduled a formal hearing for the motion of parental interference and informed my son's father visitation would resume on the next scheduled date or he'd be cited for contempt and adjourned the court.

Kathryn let me know she'd dropped her documents off at Jennifer's law office. Two days passed and Jennifer called to ask me if I forgot there was a package for me. I explained the case to her.

"You know what, I'll take a look at it" she said.

"Wonderful," I replied, "that would be great, thanks."

I called Kathryn at work but she was out at a meeting, however, the lady answering the phone said, "Can I help you? I'm Kathryn's mother."

"Well, I suggest you and your family say a prayer. A lawyer is reviewing your daughter's case and they'll let me know their decision in a day or two."

"Oh thank you so much I'll tell Kathryn you called," she said.

I have no idea why I suggested the family pray. It just came out of my mouth. The next few days were hectic. Jennifer called me to come to her office and discuss the case.

Jennifer asked if I'd met the woman. I had not. She asked how Kathryn sounded over the phone, "Fine, normal, but very scared about losing custody of her child."

"Where does Kathryn work?"

"She and her family own a printing company in the suburbs."

"Why don't you set up an appointment so the two of us can pay her a visit. Maybe we can barter for printing services in exchange for legal work?"

We met with Kathryn. Jennifer agreed to take the case in exchange for some printing services for both the legal office and my agency needs. Jennifer's strategy was simple: because Kathryn now had legal representation, the appeal for custody would go away. The other side wasn't going to spend the time and money.

On the ride back to our offices I mentioned to Jennifer there was something oddly familiar about Kathryn that I couldn't quite put my finger on. During our meeting every other word out of Kathryn and her mother's mouth seemed to be about God.

Jennifer mentioned the Christian artwork hanging on the office walls at Kathryn's.

After we parted for the day I didn't think about this anymore. I was busy preparing for a speech I was to give to a women's business association on divorce and parenting.

Standing in front of the group the next day I asked the audience to consider the following:

> When two people begin a new relationship, it is as though Cinderella and her prince have stepped out of the childhood story book we all read as kids. A more realistic way to look at it is to think of it as two people who are running for office, campaigning to be in the other person's life. Forget for a moment these two people who fall in love will change later on in the relationship. At first they'll be too busy getting the other person to "choose us" so we can

204

live happily ever after. There are often bad habits early on in a relationship we never see. For instance, leaving dirty clothes scattered, or drinking directly out of the juice carton, or maybe putting a dirty knife back in the drawer because washing is too much effort. Both sides hide their bad habits when they begin dating, because they are too busy running for the highest office in the country, ultimately the office of marriage and parenthood. This fantasy quickly fades as people grow together in a relationship. Unfortunately, about sixty percent grow apart during marriage. When the marriage ends it is like a house set on fire. All the desired hopes, dreams, and commitments cherished by both sides go up in smoke. But, we forget that the child of this relationship has yet to lay the foundation of their lives. Divorce, at any level, is devastating. For children, their warm, safe world is suddenly shattered, like a broken toy, in pieces. When parents begin to divorce, do they really stop and think about the children? All too often the children fall under the invisible heading of "power base" or worse yet, negotiable. A child's life during a divorce is like a roller coaster, going up one minute and down the next. Parents are keeping score of their child's affections as though they were at a sporting event. Both parents fear losing ground as their competition, the other parent, chips away at their own individual "power base." This is an automatic reaction during a divorce. If only parents would stop for a minute and realize that children have unconditional love for each of their parents, and remember that children were not beamed down from space to earth, but conceived and brought into this world with the greatest expectations, and most of all by love, by the two people the child calls mother and father.

These two people forget that being a parent, a role model, and a teacher means not putting down the other, or using the children to emotionally beat up the competition, because being a parent is a privilege!

A divorce is like a funeral. Unfortunately, I speak from personal experience. Of course, there is no casket or service, but the process is the same. Funeral services begin when the parties enter their lawyer's office, (I call them legal funeral representatives) they help prepare for the death of their client's marriage. The lawyer seeks out personal and confidential information about you, only to file the details in a public record for the world to see. Attached to this public record is a detailed financial description (yours) of personal property and assets acquired during the marriage. Somewhere between page eleven or fifteen of the divorce agreement, your children are listed, like assets, by name and age. And on yet another page you will find an entire section entitled *Children*, stating who gets custody when, on what days, with specific times, and for how long. We can't forget the holiday schedules, this appears on yet another page of the divorce decree. This page looks more like a major event schedule, trading odd and even years during holidays. If parents would think for a moment and get off their "power base," they would be able to work out these very private details among themselves. Months, and in some cases years later a judge, whom I refer to as the coroner (no disrespect intended) sit before strangers, in a court of law, with people whom once vowed to love, honor, and cherish each other all the days of their lives. Finally, with the tap of his gavel, the judge signs the death certificate, more commonly known as the divorce decree. I, for one, think this process is a crime. We allow total strangers to settle our once very happy lives. The greater crime, however, is the child divided up among the parents like a piece of property.

Afterwords people in attendance lined up for the book signing. A crowd of women waited patiently to have their copy of *Defending Our Lives* signed. I was surprised to see Kathryn at the luncheon. She asked if it would be alright to wait around until I was finished, she wanted to speak with me. Unfortunately, Kathryn and I didn't have an opportunity to talk. I asked her to call me later.

When I returned to the office Kathryn called, "Can we still meet?" she asked.

"Yes," I replied. "How about I meet you in an hour over at Yankee's Grill?"

We met and talked a bit about her case. I found her knowledge of books and history fascinating. She shifted the subject and began talking about the time she spent away at Pine Trail Camp in Michigan and how it changed her life, bringing her closer to God. Surprised, I mentioned this was the same camp I attended as kid.

As we continued talking she opened her purse and placed a small box on the table. With a smile on her face, Kathryn opened the box and took out a folded piece of paper. She handed it to me, "Open it up and read it."

I could hardly believe my eyes. Printed in my handwriting was my name and address. I exclaimed, "You were the girl with the red hair? I remember we'd exchanged addresses so we could keep in contact with one another."

"Susan, I had a feeling we knew each other and when I saw you in person at my office I was sure," she said.

"What are the chances of this happening?" I remarked.

"Well I believe in divine providence. God has reunited us." I didn't know if I agreed with Kathryn's theory, dismissing our reunion as nothing more than a coincidence. In fact, to be quite honest, her notion was not one I shared.

From that day forward though we embarked on a friendship. Each time we'd talk she would try and explain her abusive marriage. Each time I would change the subject, politely suggesting Kathryn seek the services of a therapist.

In dealing with people's crises and dramas almost 24/7 taking a break from time-to-time was important. I'd started going to church with Kathryn and her daughter. I was reminded of the church I attended as a kid. There were father's affectionately holding their children in their laps, husbands and wives sitting as couples. A few weeks later Kathryn's mother invited me to their house after church for Sunday lunch.

"Susan, please come, my Mom's a great cook."

I agreed to go.

I was pleasantly surprised as I stepped into the modest brick home. One wall in the living room was adorned with family photo's arranged in order from the youngest to the oldest child. The opposite wall was covered with pictures of the fifteen grandchildren. The aroma of a heavenly home-cooked meal warmed my heart. I missed the love my mother put into everything she did for me.

My mother could cook. From homemade cakes and pies, biscuits from scratch with a side of honey, to matzo ball soup, and salmon patties that melted in your mouth. I was excited to have a real home-cooked meal.

Kathryn's mother came out of the kitchen, still in her Sunday dress and an apron. "Susan, welcome to our home" she said, gently hugging me. "I hope you're hungry, from the looks of it you could use a few extra pounds. Come on into the kitchen and talk to me as I finish making lunch. Wasn't that a wonderful sermon today?"

"Yes, yes it was," I replied.

Where do you go to church she inquired."

"I don't belong to a church."

She told me she hoped I'd consider attending their church. Kathryn's mother handed me a huge bowl of whipped mashed potatoes, "Can you please," placing the oversized bowl in my hands, "put this on the table for me?"

I was ready to dig right in when Kathryn's father cleared his throat. He looked directly at me like a father scolding his child, "Shall we all hold hands, bow our heads, and give thanks to God?"

After a short prayer, I filed my plate with biscuits, mashed potatoes, and vegetables. She really did cook just like my mother.

"Kathryn, Susan forgot the meat, can you pass her the platter?"

"No thank you, I don't eat meat. I'm a vegetarian." I said.

"You don't eat meat? Well no wonder you're so skinny," commented her mother.

I really savored the meal. I had seconds, then thirds of the biscuits and potatoes.

"Susan," her mother asked, "you're not one of those people who eat and get sick are you?"

"Mother," Kathryn said, "what a terrible question to ask."

"Well, Kathryn, she's eaten all those biscuits, but from her looks she doesn't look like she ever eats."

"I ate them because they were so good. I haven't tasted food like this since my mother was alive." I explained.

We cleared the dishes and had a homemade cinnamon cake and coffee. I thanked Kathryn's mother for a lovely meal.

"Oh wait, I almost forgot," her mother said and ran into the kitchen. She returned with a bag of leftover fresh biscuits, potatoes, and cake for me. She hugged me, kissed my cheek, and said, "please try and join us for Sunday lunch again. I'll always have a place set for you at our table."

Chapter Fifteen
Ice Cold

During the next two years I continued going to battle with my son's father, spending more time on court matters than with Vincent.

The few times Vincent and I were together it was similar to a person catching up with an old friend. His father closely monitored any contact I had. As an example, if I showed up at my son's basketball game without calling to ask permission his father would climb around the bleachers in the gym and confront me, "Susan, Vincent will be upset if he sees you. He won't be able to play properly. You know you should've called, if you're smart you'll leave before I make an embarrassing scene in front of all these witnesses."

"Can I say hello to Vincent first, give him a kiss and a hug?"

"No Susan, just leave now before he sees you and before you make me do something you'll regret."

Vincent's weight had ballooned to an unhealthy and dangerous level. We barely spent ten hours together every month and I was rarely given the opportunity to speak to him when I called.

When I'd asked his father to stop playing these games he would respond with a devilish laugh and say, "No way, go screw yourself."

I was unable to discuss this with anyone. Jennifer didn't understand because she had no children. I didn't talk about this with my other friends because I felt helpless.

When I'd get into a funk about my son, I'd think about my mother, if she were still alive none of this would've happened. We'd be someplace far away—my mother, my son, and me. I viewed her murder as a devastating tornado, a violent storm removing everything in its path. I continued to punish myself, taking responsibility for not being able to save her. The tune "if only," often played in my head.

Kathryn broached the subject of my son one time and I nearly chewed off her head. She told me, "Susan just trust God. Someday your son will be old enough to understand the truth, he will be back in your life."

"Oh Kathryn, that's so easy for you to say, you have your child. You can't tell me if the tables were reversed you'd still be saying to pray and trust God."

"Yes, I would, Kathryn said.

I ripped her a new behind, "No you wouldn't! This hasn't happened to you! I remember when you told me that if you'd ever lost your daughter during your custody case, you wouldn't know what to do? You'd be devastated. For several months you were aware of my personal hell with the courts and I know you can't sit there and say to me you'd feel the same way when you've never been tested the way I have been by almighty God."

"Susan let me speak! God asks us to trust Him. He promises to be with us as we go through these trials and assures us that whatever the results are, they are for our own good and His glory. When you look back you'll see that God was there all along."

"Really?" I began, "What the hell does that have to do with Vincent being taken from me? You're telling me this was God's plan? Removing my son from my life is a lesson I needed to learn and in time I will see? Kathryn, that makes no sense! And don't start talking about people from the Bible who've been dead for thousands of years."

Kathryn didn't back down, "Susan maybe that's what God is trying to get you to understand. You know that He loves Vincent more than you do. The Bible gives us a clear message as to who Jesus is and how we can live our lives by obeying God and resting in Him. God loves you just the way you are, but He wants your heart. If you believe in him and his word, he will radically change your life and you will know Him. I have a feeling that you've always known that God has been with you all along, yet, you don't have the faith to trust His plan for you."

I stared at her in disbelief. What she said may as well have been in a foreign language. "Are you serious? Ever since I can remember, God has never answered me. I believe in God, but I have little faith in his methods and outcome." I looked down at my watch, "Kathryn I'm late for a meeting! Maybe we'll revisit this conversation some other time."

I was furious as I got in the car. I started asking myself, "Where was God while my mother was being brutalized? Where was God when I asked him to help us get away from my father? Where was God all the times when I needed him the most?"

I continued to question the omnipresence of God, keeping uncertainty and disbelief in miracles to myself. The question really began to tug at me though. Could God exist? The Bible says He does. People say God lives in their heart and gives them hope. But what do you do if hope is never in your grasp? I had never bathed in hope, only fear. I wondered if that was the reason I had such a difficult time following and believing the teachings of God as a road map for my life. I did believe that God sent and sacrificed his son for us and, "that whosoever believeth in him should not perish, but have everlasting life." All the same, it was hard for me to keep my faith with everything that had happened to me.

The following morning there was a certified letter waiting for me in the office from the Women's Illinois Bar Association. It read: "We are pleased to inform you that you are the recipient of this year's 'Woman with Vision Award' for your work on behalf of woman and children. In your honor a dinner will be held at the Palmer House Hotel." I called Jennifer and shared the news.

"I think you might be the first non-attorney to be recognized with this award," she told me.

I wanted to prepare a speech at the award banquet about divorce, abuse, and parental alienation but Jennifer thought it would be career suicide.

"Why's that?" I asked, "won't there be judges and lawyers there? It's the perfect opportunity?"

"Susan, a banquet isn't a court for public opinion. You can't make remarks regarding your divorce case." Jennifer managed to talk me into preparing a speech about my work and those I have assisted.

The event was well attended and I spoke about my agency and how those in the room could respond to my "call to action" by volunteering their time to take one battered woman's case a year.

Afterwards several lawyers and I made a night of it on the town at a few local jazz clubs.

The next morning Jennifer called, "Like I thought, Kathryn's ex-husband withdrew his petition in court to challenge the ruling on the child custody case. Can you call Kathryn and give her the good news."

"Alright, I'll see you later," I said.

I'd not spoken with Kathryn since we'd our little blowout. When I gave her the news she was overjoyed. "Hey, you're not still angry with me, are you?" Kathryn asked.

"No, I've just been buried in work."

"Great, why don't you come over to my mom's for dinner and we'll celebrate our victory?"

"Sorry Kathryn, I can't, I have a date."

"With who?" she asked.

"I don't know, someone my girlfriend is fixing me up with, he's from out-of-town or something."

Halfway through the day, the retirement center, where my grandmother lived, called to say she had passed away.

I tried to track down my sister Patricia but she was on vacation in Mexico and wouldn't be returning, according to her office, for two weeks.

Patricia and I had remained apart once I began helping abused women and sharing our parent's story publicly.

My grandmother's friends and relatives had all passed on themselves so there was no one left to contact. I wasn't going to wait until my sister returned to make arrangements, so I called my girlfriend, explaining why I had to cancel our plans and reschedule meeting the mystery man for another time.

Since my girlfriend was Jewish I asked her opinion about burying my grandmother. Sarah informed me "the proper burial lies with the next of kin and Jewish law requires the deceased's children to go to great lengths to respect the departed's wishes. It's believed that since the soul has now arrived to the world of truth it surely sees the value of a proper Jewish burial, and administering a traditional Jewish burial is actually granting what the person truly wishes at the moment."

"So if I have her cremated is it against Jewish law? I asked.

"You got it."

Even with this advice I hadn't decided what to do about my grandmother. On my way to the hospital to meet the Chaplin a call came in from a suburban police department, the intern at the office said they wanted to know if I could meet with a woman who was in serious danger. I made a U-turn on the highway and headed the opposite direction of the hospital to meet with the woman.

An hour later I arrived at an oversized multi-level apartment property. Lights were flashing on the dash boards of unmarked squad cars parked curb side at the front of the complex.

A young woman, Donna, in her early twenties sat in an oversized chair, still trembling. Paramedics were checking the kids for injuries.

Her husband, who was the property maintenance man, had tried to kill his wife, Donna, when she discovered he'd been stealing money and jewelry from tenants to pay for his drug habit.

The police had located a sawed off shotgun in the boiler room of the building and they were canvassing the area, searching for him. A detective took me into the hallway and explained the situation.

I squatted down to where Donna was sitting and introduced myself, placing my hands over hers, "It's going to be alright. We're making arrangements to move you to a safe location." She was too upset to communicate.

I rose and went into the kitchen to bring her some water. I opened the fridge and there was barely any food inside and I noticed bottles of insulin on the shelf.

As I handed her a glass of water I asked, "are you diabetic?"

I looked over at the detective and said, "maybe someone can go get her something to eat before she goes into shock."

He agreed and sent one of his men out for food. A little girl ran out from the bedroom to her mother. I could also hear a baby crying and walked into the kid's room and picked the baby girl up from the crib. With the little girl in my arms, I said, "Donna, I'm going to have to ask you some questions."

I learned that her husband planned to kill her because she was going to testify against him for a string of home invasions. It was clear she and her kids were not going to be able to remain in the apartment.

"Detective can you see about a hotel voucher for a few days until I can get her placed somewhere?"

"Yes, we should be able to do that," he replied.

"Okay Donna, I need you to pack a bag for you and the kids. Do you have enough diapers?" I asked.

She responded no. I made a list of things to pick up at the store. I stayed with her until she was transported to a hotel a few miles away.

The detective arranged for a State's Attorney to interview the young mother at the hotel.

After dropping Donna off, and on my way to getting supplies, I detoured to the hospital to take care of the necessary paperwork on my grandmother.

At the hospital the Chaplin asked me if I had made arrangements yet with a funeral home.

I replied, "No, not yet."

The Chaplain told me, "A Rabbi was here earlier to pray over the body. You seem out of sorts, why don't we go into my office or to the chapel and talk. Death of a loved one is often overwhelming," said the Chaplin.

I told the Chaplin I was fine. He asked me if I wanted to be with my grandmother to say goodbye, "No," I responded, "we weren't really that close."

I looked down at my watch, "I really have to be going, is there anything else you need from me?"

The Chaplin stood before me, perplexed, "Pardon me ma'am, but this isn't how I'd expected you to react. My job is to spend time with grieving families and, frankly, given what I know you do for so many others I'm perplexed by your coldness."

Foul ball, I thought to myself then said, "My grandmother's passing has nothing to do with what I do. I think, you sir, are out of line to make such a bold statement. If there's nothing more, I need to be going."

I felt like I had just been scolded. Once in my car I held a conversation with my three favorite people—me, myself, and I. Telling myself things I wish I had said to the rude Chaplin.

I loaded the car with supplies that would help Donna for a few days and went to the hotel where a detective had remained until I arrived. I sat with Donna and wrote case notes, personal information, and who to contact in case of emergency. I explained she would need to obtain a criminal order of protection.

"I'm afraid that will only make him angrier," she replied.

"Why don't you let me worry about that for now," I told her. As I finished up, the detective was giving Donna instructions on what to do if her husband contacted her.

"There will be an officer posted outside the door until morning, so and your children will be safe. Here is my card if you need anything."

The detective and I left at the same time. "Hey I'm hungry and I hate eating alone, want to stop and get something to eat?" he asked me.

I agreed and followed him to a bar and grill a mile or so up the road. We sat at a booth on the far end of the bar and ordered. Jack was a handsome man in his early forties with thick hair the color of dark coal and piercing, deep set brown eyes.

"You're quite attractive in person. Those television cameras don't do you justice. And you have a gorgeous mane of hair. Are you seeing anyone?" Jack inquired.

"Um, well," I stuttered.

"A simple yes or no works," he said with a smile.

I looked down at my watch, "I really have to be going," as I signaled the waitress to bring over the check. Jack reached across the table and grabbed my hand.

"I'm not taking no for answer."

I knew this was a bad idea and nervously I shook my leg up and down, you could hear my shoe tapping on the floor. Jack reached under the table to calm my nervous shake. I never did well with men one-on-one. I was afraid of the intimacy, terrified they would discover I was damaged goods. Fearful my secret would be revealed. I didn't know how to let down my guard. I had no clue what it meant to give myself to a person completely. I used humor and quick wit to disguise my inability to relate in a relationship. Finally I said, "I'm allergic to men with badges. In fact, I took an oath never to date anyone in law enforcement."

Jack laughed, "Really? Who are you kidding? A cop is what I do to earn a living. It doesn't define who I am. I attend church weekly, I'm into gardening, I'm one hell of a lover, and I've been searching for a woman like you for a long time. Don't punish me because I happen to be a cop like your dad, we're not all cut from the same cloth."

In my head I heard the words, "Danger, danger," similar to the robot from the television program *Lost in Space*. The robot would light up, spin around, and warn the make-believe Robinson family of imminent dangers.

I took a deep breath before responding, "I can't go out with you," and placed the money on the table to cover the check, got up and left to go home.

I could hear Jack calling me back to the table. In the parking lot, I was so shaken I fumbled with my car keys trying to unlock my car.

The keys slipped from my hand onto the gravel lot. From out of nowhere Jack reached down and picked up the keys. As he started to return the keys to me, he jerked his hand back, "Why don't you at least give it some thought?" Then he moved towards me, adding, "I would really like the opportunity to get to know you."

Gently, he kissed my cheek. I opened my car door, sat down, and started the car. As I drove home all I could think about was Jack. Was he for real? Or maybe I just presented a challenge, something he merely wanted, a prize you win at a carnival after hitting the bull's eye.

I tried, but I couldn't get past the fact that Jack was a cop, and this was a deal breaker for me.

I finally decided to have my grandmother cremated. By the time my sister returned from vacation my grandmother's ashes were ready.

Patricia was furious with me for not giving Grandma a proper Jewish burial. "What was I suppose to do? You were out of town. I didn't have much choice" I said.

"Susie, you knew Grandma wanted a proper Jewish burial."

"Fine, Patricia, come and pick up her ashes so you can take them to the cemetery and bury them in her cemetery plot next to Grandpa."

We made arrangements to meet. I handed her the urn. Patricia gave me a kiss and said goodbye in a tone that meant I would never see or speak to her again.

Later that day I prepared to attend a formal gala at the Fairmont Hotel where I was scheduled to introduce the singer Michael Bolton who was performing to raise money on behalf of sexually abused children.

It was a big event, even the Governor and Mayor Daley were in attendance. After introducing Michael Bolton, I stood off stage as he performed, watching along with members of his security detail and staff. Suddenly, someone's hands covered my eyes, "guess who," said the voice.

I turned around into Jack's arm's. "Come with me." he whispered as he lead me up the stairs, over the catwalk directly above the stage.

"My God, you're absolutely stunning," he said as he drew me closer to him. We danced on the catwalk as Michael Bolton sang, "When a man loves a woman."

My eyes filled with tears. The emotional words in the song and being in Jack's arms was a magical moment. We continued dancing long after the music stopped.

Slowly, Jack brought his face close to mine as if he were about to kiss me, but instead he whispered in my ear, suggesting we leave and go someplace else.

The next thing I remember we had pulled into Jack's driveway. He'd opened a bottle of Merlot and we continued dancing in the living room to Carol King's, "I feel the earth move under my feet." That wasn't all that was moving around that night.

Our bodies stayed connected through mid-afternoon the next day. "I don't want to move, but nature calls, and I'm starving," I announced to Jack.

He threw me a robe and we raided the refrigerator. We spent the weekend together. Finally, Jack drove me home, but we didn't want it to end so he stayed until morning.

"Oh, I really don't want to go to work." I said.

Jack suggested we both call in sick and play for the day, but I just couldn't. I had a luncheon presentation to give at a club downtown.

Jack called almost every hour on the hour leaving messages, "I miss you, call me when you can."

The day got away from me with women needing assistance and the media requesting commentary from me regarding a shooting on the west side which involved a woman and her former boyfriend.

Jack and I made plans to meet up later that evening. When I arrived home there was a bouquet of roses on the doorstep. The note said, "Miss you baby—Jack."

Jack became too clingy. I figured that once we passed the mushy stage in the relationship he'd settle down.

Two weeks after we'd begun seeing each other Jack handed me the key to his house. He talked of wanting to get married. Things were moving too fast. I tried to put some distance between us, it was useless. When Jack didn't hear from me during the day, he'd wait at my house until I got home.

"Come on this is crazy, why don't we just get married?" he asked.

As wonderful as Jack was, he was exhibiting all the characteristics of a controlling and jealous man. I added additional days to my trip to New Mexico and said nothing until the morning he drove me to the airport.

I told him, after the conference, I would be staying a few extra days with a girlfriend. Two days before I was to return home, Jack flew into town and called me from a hotel in Santa Fe. "Surprise Baby, I couldn't wait to see you."

I didn't react the way I wanted to, instead I acted as though I was happy to see him. I knew that once we returned home, figuring out how to end the relationship wasn't going to be easy. But, I didn't have a choice. I don't know if I just wasn't ready for a serious relationship, or if his behavior scared me. Either way when I finally ended the relationship Jack fell apart, begging me for another chance.

I accompanied Donna to court for another order of protection, afterwards we met with the State's Attorney who had issued a warrant for her husband's arrest. When the meeting ended, I drove her back to her apartment which had been donated by a landlord. Donna was looking in to returning to school and getting a nursing degree, but she had a long way to go before she could apply for school.

The legal paperwork required was going to take several months before legal aid agreed to take her divorce and custody case pro bono. The criminal case remained in limbo because her husband was in hiding.

When the divorce was finalized, Donna was granted sole custody, we worked on getting her public assistance. Donna enrolled in college under a brand new identity.

Once Donna moved out-of-state, for her own safety, she was no longer able to communicate with anyone back home. Her situation was too dangerous. Any calls made to relatives went through a third party relay service and all correspondence was directed through a safe, mail routing address we'd set up. Her husband never surfaced, leading police to conclude he fled to Canada or Mexico.

Chapter Sixteen
Not in My Sandbox

The following week, after I stopped seeing Jack, Kathryn and I had a girl's evening at her house. I made dinner and we watched movies. "I was thinking, next time you start dating a guy, you should take things slower," suggested Kathryn.

Then she pointed out my track record. "For someone who teaches women how to pick the right man, you're not one to follow your own advice."

Kathryn had the best of intentions, I'm sure, but I was in no mood to listen to another sermon. I agreed with her and changed the subject.

The next day I ran into my girlfriend Sarah, "Hey, when do you have time to get together so I can fix you up with that blind date?"

I told her it didn't matter, my schedule was open. About this same time, a law firm approached me to participate in a new business to provide resources and written materials to corporations on violence in the workplace.

I met with the partners of the prestigious thirty-year-old law firm. I didn't tell anyone, not even Jennifer about the proposed venture.

After two months of talks they were ready to move forward with the project. A new company was created called Corporate-On-Site, Inc., and I was expected to work in their offices.

I had shares in the company and we negotiated contracts to begin in the spring. I didn't know how to break the news to Jennifer. I desperately needed to generate a steady income, living from hand-to-mouth was becoming far too exhausting for me.

Once the deal was completed, I decided to let the agency Project: Protect go. I retained the high risk clients who required continued support and services but officially stopped taking any new case's a month before my move.

I rehearsed what I'd say to Jennifer. I knew she wasn't going to be happy with my decision. Forty percent of her firm's yearly revenue came directly from my work with women requiring skilled divorce and child custody representation.

After disclosing my plans, Jennifer was irrate. "After everything we've worked on you do this to me! You're stabbing me in the back! If you move forward with this project I'm going to pull out of your son's custody case."

"Wait," I responded, "you're going to stop representing me in my custody case because I've decided that eating and having a steady income is important to my survival? I've brought in hundreds of thousands of dollars and media to your firm! Have you ever once offered me a paid gig as a consultant or case manager in the firm? No and why is that? How the hell am I suppose to live and pay my bills!" I shouted back.

"You should've thought about this before you agreed to sign your fucking deal," cried Jennifer.

"What you're saying is if I drop this deal you'll continue to represent me in court and we'll remain friends?"

"That's what I said."

"Jennifer that's blackmail"

"No Susan, it's called business."

"I see, so our friendship isn't what I thought, it's been about business and how many dollars I don't benefit from that I bring in your door each month."

"No," replied Jennifer, "I don't charge you for being the attorney for the agency and for being your personal lawyer. It's a wash in the end."

"A wash? How is that possible?" I rattled off the amount of retainer fees and monthly income she received from what she termed a wash. "And you haven't done shit in my custody case except shuffle paper."

Jennifer cleared her throat, "Well then, you have 24 hours to consider my terms, otherwise take your ass out those doors and do not return."

I stormed out of her office. Then I called Kathryn asking what I should do. We met up later that evening.

"Susan, Jennifer showed you her true colors. You seem to have a habit of getting attached to controlling people and this is just another abusive situation."

"Kathryn, I don't know what to do?" I replied.

"I can't tell you what to do. Only point out that Jennifer's behavior seems like someone incapable of being a true friend."

I stayed up most of the night pacing back and forth in my living room, trying to find an answer. Maybe I'd remained friends with Jennifer because she'd given me a sliver of hope that I might regain custody of my son.

I'd still not learned how to stay away from controlling, manipulative people. Or perhaps I emitted some invisible scent only detectable to those who figured out it's code—similar to battered women who continue to be involved with abusers.

Finally I made up my mind and ended all contact with Jennifer. I searched for another lawyer to represent me in my ongoing custody case. I was so tired of the games people played. Although I was not conscious of my actions, I knew at some level they dictated outcomes which appeared to be preventable to others, but to me they weren't. I was wearing a blindfold, always willing to give anyone who crossed my path the benefit of the doubt.

Kathryn reminded me that the Bible said to, "Be wise as a serpent and harmless as a dove."

Amongst all of this Sarah called to remind me we were meeting the following evening at a restaurant downtown with her boyfriend Joe and his friend, Paul.

"Oh, and Susan, try not to be late. I expect to see you at 7:00 o'clock sharp."

Another mystery date. The last time I agreed to be fixed up by Sarah the guy was short, bald, and boring. He picked at the hairs in his nose when he thought no one was paying attention. I walked into the noisy bar at 7 PM and spotted Sarah and Joe waving me over. Joe rose from his seat as did his friend.

All I noticed was his friend's bright and welcoming smile as I walked to the table. Sarah made the introductions. Joe's friend, Paul, said, "it's a pleasure to meet you," as he kissed my hand.

I laughed so hard during dinner my sides ached. Paul was both charming and witty. As the evening wore on I couldn't separate his humor, self-confidence, and conceit. Paul certainly was colorful in his usage of words. Joe said he was a talented builder. Maybe Paul's attitude was common of men in the construction trade, but something about him made me smile from the inside.

When we concluded our evening, Paul asked where I was going, "home to bed, I have an early start in the morning."

"Great," he replied, "where are we meeting for breakfast?" he asked.

"You're pretty sure of yourself," I remarked.

"Always," he replied.

"Okay, Paul, let's meet at Lou's around 6:30 for breakfast," I said.

I thanked Paul for a lovely evening and headed home.

An hour later, my cell phone rang, "Did you miss me?" asked the voice. "It's Paul, I wanted to call and make sure you made it home safe, I'll see you in a few hours for breakfast."

Around three in the morning my pager went off. I dressed and responded to a client in distress. Her car had broken down and she had no one else to call. I called a tow truck service and took her back home. She had turned her life around after leaving a dangerous husband by going to school and holding down a full-time job at a medical clinic. I was happy to have spent some time with her and hearing about her progress.

Exhausted, I called Paul and left a message that I'd had an emergency and couldn't meet him for breakfast. I finished some paperwork and checked out my new office at the law firm.

After a lunch meeting, one of the lawyers asked how Jennifer took the news about our exciting new venture. I explained that Jennifer wasn't supportive. The lawyer offered to intervene if I needed files or documents from Jennifer's office.

Paul called several times, but I was too busy to call him back. When I got home Paul had left several funny messages on my voice mail saying he was heading back to Wisconsin.

Although I was busy setting up the new business, Paul and I talked on the phone nearly every day. Paul wanted to see me again. What attracted me to Paul was his rugged sense of self and his raw usage of words. He'd say things that other people would probably find crude, but for some reason I found his commentaries harmless and bold.

After a few months of talking on the phone, he didn't ask, but stated, very matter-of-factly, "I'll be in Chicago over the weekend to meet with Joe on a project and then I'll pick you up for dinner. I hope to see you dressed in the highest pair of heels you own and the hottest shade of red lipstick you can find."

I hung up the phone and thought about his request and laughed out loud. A former neighbor, who happened to be my sister's Godmother called asking if I could meet her to talk. I couldn't but asked if she could just talk to me over the phone.

She was hesitant, insisting I meet with her in person.

"I'm sorry, no, I just don't have any time right now. Please whatever it is can't you tell me over the phone? Is it your husband, the kids what?" I asked.

"Susie, I'm really not comfortable talking about this over the phone." After several minutes of back and forth over the phone, she blurted out, "It's Andy, my youngest, he's well, under the care of a psychiatrist and uh, I don't know how to…he, is being treated for depression and suicide."

I responded by saying I was sorry to hear about Andy and I wished him a speedy recovery.

"Susie, that's only part of why I'm calling, the doctor thought you could come in and meet with him."

"But why, for what reason?" I asked.

"This is the hard part, because, well, it has to do with your father," she replied.

When she finally explained, I was speechless. It seems that when Andy was younger my father would lure him and another neighbor boy into the basement of our house and perform various sexual acts with them.

I was gone and out of the house by this time and didn't know what to say. I didn't question her claims, I fully believed they were valid. What she told me wasn't something a person made up. I explained I needed to think about what she'd said for a day or so and then I'd call her back.

Before I hung up I asked her not to mention this to my sister, Patricia. "Too late," she responded, "my daughter already told her."

"Jesus Marian Joseph," I shouted, "why would you tell her that?"

"Because Andy needs help and we called her first."

"Okay, give me a little time and I'll call you back."

Unfortunately this all made sense. It never crossed my mind until then, but the pieces to the missing puzzle fell into place. My father had sexually abused my sweet brother Bobby too. That's what he meant, years ago, when we were having lunch after the death of my parents in the restaurant and he'd wondered why, "I didn't take him with me when I left."

What my father had done triggered my brother's mental illness. My father was not only a murderer, he was a serial pedophile.

A swell of emotion and anger came over me. I wanted all of this to go away. With my legs folded Indian style, I rocked back and forth on my living room floor, sick to my stomach.

The call about Andy was a bombshell, bringing back what I'd tried to forget. The memories of what my father had done to me now played in my head like a bad movie. "Jesus Christ, can't people leave things be," I screamed out loud. I just couldn't deal with it, I shut down for the weekend.

I spent the next few days wondering who else might be a victim? Did he do this to other children in the neighborhood?

I avoided calling my former neighbor back because, frankly, I didn't know what to say. She continued to call though.

Finally, my sister left a voice message demanding I return this ladies call. This was the final straw, angry that Patricia was now calling me too. I made the call, the answering machine clicked on and I said, "This is Susan Murphy, I'm sorry but please don't call me again there is nothing I'm able to do for your son."

Unfortunately, she didn't see it that way and continued to contact me, demanding I meet with her son's doctor. She also figured my father had done the same thing to me.

This was none of her business. I was not prepared to deal with these issues. It was easier to hide from the truth and rebury the pain as far as I was concerned.

Finally, I changed my telephone number. Again, someone else wanted me to own their pain and suffering. I was strong enough by then to refuse ownership of yet another dark toy in someone else's sandbox of life. My sandbox was full.

For the next several weeks I went searching the streets of Chicago for my brother. He was nowhere to be found.

Chapter Seventeen
Giddy Up

When the door buzzer rang, I hit the speaker button and heard, "it's Paul, let me in."

Oh shit, I forgotten all about him.

I opened the door and heard Paul say, "hey you're not dressed for dinner."

"Okay, and you are?" I responded. "Since when does a shirt with pictures of swimming fish, carpenter shorts, and construction boots scream anything other than a commercial for a Jerry Springer episode?"

"That's unfair," Paul remarked, "I do have all my teeth."

We laughed.

I poured him a drink and we talked. Since we weren't going out for dinner I handed him a takeout menu and we ordered Thai.

After dinner, in the living room we danced to Tony Bennett and Lena Horne. I refreshed his drink. With one arm, Paul pulled my chair closer to him, "that's better, now I can see you."

I giggled like a school girl.

When I asked what hotel he was staying at he said "I'm not, I thought I was staying here tonight. Besides, I've had too much to drink to get behind the wheel of a car."

I made up the couch for him. When I came out of the bathroom, Paul was in his t-shirt and underwear passed out in my bed. I found myself watching Paul sleep. His full head of perfectly cut, reddish brown hair framed his rugged face. He was handsome even as he slept.

I tried to get into bed without waking him, then again who knew if he was really sleeping? He rolled over to where I was like a slithering snake. Using the strength of his hands and forearms Paul drew me closer to him and started speaking.

His tone was hypnotic and masculine. I could listen to him talk for hours. His cologne danced in perfect harmony with his body chemistry.

Paul didn't have hair dangling from his nose or ears, he had all his teeth and he had a talent for making me laugh. Something no man had ever accomplished with any consistency. Paul's persona was a cross between John Wayne and Steve McQueen. A man's man, as they say, whose laughter and smile was contagious. Another unexpected surprise was how we exchanged intimate moments as though we'd always been together.

For the first time in my adult life, I wasn't afraid of getting close to a man. Paul had a way of making me feel good about myself as a women.

We remained comfortable, nestled in another arms, until I heard the sounds of Paul's rumbling stomach. We dressed and went out for breakfast. Arm in arm we strolled along Grant Park, then back to my place where we undressed and climbed back into bed, soaking in the warmth of one another's arms, dozing on and off.

When I finally asked what time Paul was going back to Wisconsin, he declared he wanted to stay over another night.

I told him that was impossible I had to get ready for an awards dinner. He said I should've told him, he would've brought a suit.

"No, I'm being picked up, you can't stay," I said.

He didn't seem too pleased with the idea that I had a date, but, I explained, I wasn't to blame. Before the weekend had started I didn't anticipate any of this happening.

Paul said he did. He knew from the moment we met.

I excused myself and went into the shower. When I came out Paul was still in bed with a smile that lit up the room.

"Come on, you have to be on your way, I need to get ready." I told him.

Paul asked, "When will I see you again?"

"I'm not sure."

Paul demanded we figure it out. Then called the train station. When I asked what he was doing, he said I was dropping him off at the station with his truck. Then on Thursday, when I was finished with work, I could drive his truck up to Wisconsin.

Paul said he wanted to be sure I was driving a safe vehicle. I knew he thought by giving me his truck to drive I would have no excuse not to show up.

After I drove Paul to the train I hurried back and got dressed. As I was straightening up the apartment the smell of Paul's cologne overpowered the bedroom. Paul had scattered his cologne everywhere. I opened the windows hoping it would go away.

Pressed for time and because I wanted to be downstairs when my date arrived, I hurried up.

"What are you doing down here?" my date asked when he saw me waiting in the lobby.

"Well, I didn't want to be late and traffic is all backed up."

"Baby, we have plenty of time. How about we go back up and have a quiet drink before we go?" he suggested.

"Nn..noo, we can't, my girlfriend got into a fight with her husband and she's upstairs passed out on my couch so let's stop some place on the way," I stammered.

I mostly remember the evening as being very long and people talking to me about nothing of any memorable importance. The smell of Paul's cologne remained strong when I returned home.

Paul called while I was gone but I didn't call him back. I changed the sheets and pillow cases, they were laced with the cologne.

In the morning Paul called to ask if I had a good time with my date.

"Very funny, it wasn't a date," I said.

"Okay, were you picked up at your home for a prearranged evening," he asked.

"Yes," I said.

"Well then, according to the laws of life sweetheart, that's a date and I hope you had a terrible time."

"I had a great evening, thank you for asking."

That Monday I was behind in my work. I had to prepare three back-to-back lectures, each on different topics, in the next 24 hours. By the time Thursday arrived I was exhausted. After I finished up my final lecture on school children and violence, I followed Paul's hand written directions to his home in Wisconsin.

Two hours later I arrived. There was a note on the counter from Paul to make myself comfortable and that he'd be there around six.

I knew Paul built the house with his bare hands, but never imagined it would be so colorful and full of life. From the forest green counter tops and warm gold and cranberry colors, to the unique stone fireplace and the fifteen-foot high ceilings I felt as though I was home.

Walking into each bedroom made me think of Goldilocks and the three bears. When I walked into the master bedroom where "papa bear slept," I took a deep breath. Paul's scent lingered in the room like air freshener.

Waiting for him I fell asleep on top of the bed and woke to Paul's smiling face. "It's about time you got here, did you miss me?" Paul asked, then added, "Of course you did, I'm a great guy, who wouldn't miss this smile."

Paul was a fan of asking and answering his own questions. We gazed into each other's eyes like two puppy dogs in heat, as if we were meeting on a return visit at the neighborhood park. An hour later the doorbell rang.

Paul popped out of bed, "Oh I forgot, it's the boys, they won't be here long. You can't meet them naked, giddy up, put some clothes on."

Paul's friends stayed long enough to have a quick drink while staring at me with approving eyes before they were on their way. My feet didn't touch the ground the entire weekend.

On Monday morning Paul and I talked ourselves out of me returning back to Chicago for another day. Instead, he drove me around the small town that looked more like a television setting of Mayberry from the *Andy Griffith Show*.

Using Paul's truck I drove back home. But the drive back to Chicago was difficult, I didn't want to go back. The heavy rush hour traffic on the Interstate forced my mind to return to reality though.

I couldn't remember if I'd ever experienced the feeling of peace that was within me. It was like I'd permanently put on a brand new undergarment for life, or so I wanted to believe at the time.

The only drawback was that Paul drank in excess. This should've been a red flag, but it wasn't. We were married a few months later. And I moved to Wisconsin.

I didn't pay much attention at the beginning. Unlike my father, Paul didn't turn into a two-headed monster or display any signs of anger when he drank. So, I just accepted it. Each day he'd return home from work at exactly six in the evening, pour himself a glass filled with vodka and ice, then continue drinking until he fell asleep.

Paul would often remark this was his way of, "clearing the deck." Truth was, Paul was an angry man using booze like a sedative to quiet all the noise in his head so he could sleep at night. A month after we'd married, Paul's temper appeared. Add in controlling, crude, and manipulative—translation: dynamite. I'd married a live stick of explosives.

Within six to seven weeks after our marriage, Paul expected his drink to be waiting for him on the counter when he walked through the door each evening.

We'd then sit and talk, while he drank, until it was time for me to put him to bed.

My relocation to Wisconsin, after we married, was a difficult adjustment to make. I knew no one. My new life was a real culture shock, coming from big city life to what I often referred to as, "Mayberry."

The small town had very few choices in nightlife activity. You could, however, find a bar about every half mile or so, depending on the stretch of the road. And on Friday evenings most people in town went to their neighborhood bar for a greasy fish fry.

With a population of 3,401, the town had one newspaper that highlighted births, deaths, arrests, and the occasional farmer who won first prize for his pig at the fair.

It quickly became apparent that my saving grace during the first year of marriage was the contractual commitments which required me to travel a few days each week.

Usually I had to leave on Sunday for my scheduled visitation with my son, or, when his father pulled his "your son doesn't wish to see you," routine, I'd I leave early Monday morning for work and wouldn't return until mid-week.

When I returned, Paul would find ways to create an argument over nothing. If Paul didn't like a remark or if I didn't do as he asked, I'd get the silent treatment as if I were a child. If we'd had a disagreement before I left for work in Chicago, he'd completely ignore my calls while I was away. When I'd return, Paul would play his mind games, give me a peck on the cheek and say "you're in the dog house." Followed by a look that would make my stomach turn upside down.

I didn't want him upset with me. I loved Paul, or so I thought. Then again, what the heck did I know? Turns out I knew zero.

I had entered unchartered waters, swimming upstream praying the tide didn't take me away. For the life of me I couldn't understand why Paul was behaving like a child when he didn't get his way. Each time I left to go to work, Paul made me feel guilty.

Being in the construction industry, one evening when I returned home I found the entire family room covered in blue prints. Paul was putting together a development deal and although he never asked me to join him on the massive thirteen-acre single family housing development project, his behavior dictated otherwise.

"So when does your contract end?" he asked.

I looked at him wide eyed and in shock. I mumbled my reply. I recall the advice a lawyer friend of mine had given me when I married. She told me not to give up my identity. Ever.

Regrettably, I'd not listened to her wise advice. Without thinking I jumped into the deep water and kept on trying to swim with Paul.

Quietly, though, without Paul's knowledge I did continue assisting victims of abuse, as well as searching for my brother.

Also, for the first time since I'd moved to Wisconsin, I was able to convince my son into coming for a visit. His father drove him. We'd spent the day together without a hitch. Before his father picked Vincent up later that evening, he'd asked to come back. I was elated.

By this time the Internet had become important and in some cases life-saving in connecting with others who needed guidance on how to leave their abusers with their lives. Most nights, after Paul passed out, I worked on high risk cases of abuse and stalking.

Within a year, after the blue prints came into our home, the first phase of construction on the development project was underway. I was clueless about construction, housing, or property management. Paul said he needed me by his side though and that was all I needed to hear.

But this wasn't how he behaved. He wanted to control my every move. In fact, it became clear Paul was incapable of not being in control. He found a way, ever so gently, to sprinkle sugar on top of every word he spoke. He knew when and how to use compliments. While at the same time demanding to know where I was and with whom. If a stranger or acquaintance paid me a compliment, Paul was crude in his response.

When the first, multi-family building was scheduled to open I was like a lost sheep taking Paul's direction in management of the property. I learned quickly to stay out of his way. When something went wrong on the site, or with the subcontractors, he was very quick to blow up at the problem. Over time Paul's business attitude became very clear, it was, "his way or no way." His frequent mood swings often mirrored what was happening at the construction site.

In the midst of all this, we learned I was going to have a baby. For a split second, the idea of starting a brand new life, in another place, with a chance to have a family was appealing. I'd never thought about having more children, but it crossed my mind that maybe, just maybe, this was God's plan for me. More than anything, though, I was starved for a happy, normal life.

A few weeks after the news of the baby, Paul gave me a financial assignment. In my haste to do the task I made several miscalculations with the numbers and Paul began screaming at me. He informed me that he had to redo them.

It was a costly error, all of which was my fault. I was very upset and sick over the incident. Tired, I wanted to go to bed, but Paul insisted I stay up until he figured out the correct information to enter on the forms. When he finished Paul instructed me to head to the office in town where I was ordered to, "complete these forms at the office on the computer, and when you're finished, fax them out to the banks." Then he went upstairs and slammed the bedroom door.

Before I left for the office, I stepped in the bathroom and noticed some light bleeding, but I was so upset that instead of heading to the hospital, I went to the office and finished the forms.

By the time I returned home, Paul was up and out the door to work. I went straight to bed, and awoke a few hours later to find the sheets covered in blood. I dressed and drove myself to the hospital.

Once there, I wrote Paul's cell phone number on a piece of paper and asked the nurse to contact Paul and to tell him I was at the hospital. When I came out of the ultrasound, Paul was waiting for me.

I was having a miscarriage and was in a great deal of discomfort, sadness, and pain. Paul cradled my head in his lap, but said in a half kidding, partially serious tone of voice, "I guess this gets you out of the dog house for screwing up the financial forms for the bank." I was horrified by his remarks.

My God, we had just lost a child!

Chapter Eighteen
Rowing Without a Paddle

There isn't a word to describe how I felt after the miscarriage. The loss of the baby drained all my energy. Trips to the hospital for excessive bleeding kept me bed ridden.

A few days later I felt good enough to climb out of bed, shower, and get some fresh air. I put on a warm oversized jacket and with a cup of hot tea in hand sat outside on the back deck of the house. Paul's crude words at the hospital continued to weigh heavily on my mind.

I realized Paul was nothing more than a verbally abusive bully, using words that punched hard to the very core of my being. How could I love anyone like this? More and more I noticed traces of my own father in Paul. I even identified with my mother and why she had stayed with my father all those years.

The thought of missing my mom started me bawling like a little girl. More than ever I wished my mother were with me, or better yet, that I could go "up above" with her to heaven. Unfortunately, there was more truth to this than I would ever admit to anyone publicly. I even said a prayer to God asking for one wish, that He bring me home! I'd had enough of this life on earth. Without my family, most of all my son, what was the point?

I came to the realization I was living in the middle of nowhere and all of my friends were in Chicago. Foolishly, I'd cut off all my previous business ties, believing my new life would magically work out.

The days ahead were especially tough. Between new construction and renting apartments so we could pay the mortgage, I barely had time for providing services to victims of abuse.

Somehow I juggled everything until I could figure what I was going to do next. When a couple of my girlfriends from Chicago came up to spend the weekend the time didn't go as planned. Paul was in a foul mood because something had gone wrong on the construction site and he said it wasn't a good time for visitors. I didn't care, I really missed Kathryn and Maggie.

Naturally, the day my girlfriends were to arrive I was suddenly called to scramble a woman into housing who would have likely been killed by her abusive husband. Since it was the weekend, contacting a lawyer had to wait until Monday, so I placed her and her toddler in one of the new units that we were using as a model for showing apartments. I quickly settled them in, dropped off groceries, and directed them to stay put until Monday morning, explaining how important it was no one know where they were.

The thought crossed my mind that if Paul found out these two were in his new building I'd have hell to pay. Paul wasn't very supportive of what I did for battered and abused woman and children.

When Kathryn and Maggie arrived I tried to focus on our time together. When Paul walked in he was charming and funny, cracking jokes, yet under his breath he mumbled why couldn't they have chosen any time but now to show up.

Although I was mad at him, I acted as if I didn't hear what he said. I handed Paul his drink and poured wine for Maggie and Kathryn.

Two hours later Paul began slurring his words, which was my queue to jump up and get dinner on the table. I could tell by the look on Kathryn's face she was outraged.

After dinner, I declared, "Okay Paul, let's get you off to bed. Ladies I'll return momentarily."

He gave me a difficult time when I put him to bed. I prayed he'd stay out cold for the night so I could spend quality time with my girlfriends.

When I came out of the master bedroom, my friends were out on the back deck, sipping wine, smoking, and talking.

Kathryn looked at me and said, "What are you doing?"

Maggie chimed in, "Susan, we don't like what we've been witnessing all evening. You may like your dream home and all, but that guy is an abusive asshole. Oh and let's not forget that he drinks like a fish."

I sat in silence, staring at the two of them not knowing how to respond. Finally I replied with absolutely the stupidest remark I could, "I have it all under control."

I'd convinced myself that because I was not beaten with Paul's bare hands, like my mother had been, my life was different. How wrong I was! Paul's words were his weapons of mass destruction and my excuse, to make it work. If I wasn't visibly black and blue then everything in my world was under control.

"Okay so he drinks a little too much, and ..."

Kathryn interrupted, "And my God, he's a cruel man who treats you terribly. Why are you putting up with his behavior, he's a psychopathic wacko?"

I didn't have a response. I was embarrassed. Trying to make light of a serious matter brought on another hour of conversation about how I, of all people, had fallen for an abuser.

Kathryn declared, "You, of all people should know better."

I was finally able to divert the topic but it didn't change anything. They continued, through their body language and tone, to be annoyed with me.

Paul left for the job site before any of us got up the next morning. I made breakfast and the three of us hung out at the house.

Maggie decided we should drive into Madison and do some shopping. My cell phone rang, it was Paul.

"What did you do! Goddammit! Get down here immediately," click.

I tried to leave the girls at the house, but they insisted on taking a ride with me down to the apartment complex and from there we would leave and go shopping. I was not thrilled, judging from Paul's tone, I was in deep shit for something.

I hurried into the apartment office where Paul was sitting behind the desk at the computer. "Susan, have a seat."

"No, I'm okay, they're waiting in the car, what's up?" I asked.

"Sit down!" Paul handed me a print out for the rent roll then asked me to go down the tenant list with him. Halfway through when I said a unit was vacant, Paul raised his left eyebrow, leaned forward into the desk, "you sure we don't have a tenant in that unit?"

Paul shuffled papers on top of the desk then looked at me as if to say, prepare yourself for some unfriendly fire. "Susan, the rent roll sheet and computer says this unit is vacant, however, a small boy who pulled the fire alarm box about an hour ago says otherwise. How many times do I have to tell you? Keep 'those women' out of my buildings. We're not a shelter!"

I agonized in silence trying to find the words to respond with. I stood up from the chair, shrugged my shoulders, shook my head, and said the girls were waiting in the car and I'd see him back at the house later.

Finally, after three years of marriage and what seemed like a thousand's empty vodka bottles later, I was able to predict when Paul would either slip into a publicly drunken, or embarrassing mess and when I would have to say, "Let's go, time for bed."

Between Paul, the women in crisis I was trying to help, and the fight in the courts over my son, life was overwhelming.

Sleep deprived and out of emotional gas, memories that I had buried from my childhood began to surface. Whenever I fell asleep, dreams of my father chasing me down a dead end road haunted me. I continued to have reoccurring nightmare's in which I was in an underground tunnel trying to find an opening to escape. I never found an escape and would wake up, startled, in a heavy soaked sweat.

Paul's fits of rage continued to escalate. Everything and everyone seemed to set him off, including me. The only peace in my day was when I would take off his work boots and finally tuck him into bed.

The fear of not knowing what to do was paralyzing. More than anything I wanted to believe that the person who had showed up at my door a few years earlier in Chicago, with a smile bright enough to light up a room, would come back to me. Unfortunately, somewhere along the way he'd gotten lost in the sea of booze.

With financial constraints mounting, it became clear Paul was in over his head. I no longer believed him when he said, "we have to hang in just a little longer."

It would be two more years before I made the decision to leave and go back to Chicago.

The banks pulled their financial support from the construction project and Paul dug us deeper into debt, lying to his investment partners to get more money to continue.

A close associate of ten years, Daniel, severed all ties with Paul and urged me to get out before something happened to me. Daniel expressed his worries about my safety, recommending I do whatever was required.

Over coffee in a nearby town, Daniel met with me and said, "Paul, is going down. Someone is going to bury his ass."

Daniel was still reeling from when Paul had screwed him on money owed for work he'd done as a subcontractor. "I will never understand what you saw in him, never," he said to me.

I learned, many months later, that Daniel had been meeting with the United States Attorney's Office in Wisconsin to build a case against Paul.

After talking with Daniel, I headed to Chicago for the afternoon to see Kathryn and began making arrangements to leave Paul.

The coach house on her property was vacant so I agreed to rent it. She wasn't happy with my target date to leave Paul, Kathryn pressed me to leave right away. What she didn't realize at the time was that too many victims of violence depended on me for basic survival. I'd provided housing on various properties we owned in Wisconsin.

"Kathryn, you don't understand, I can't just up and leave. I've got to make sure a lot of things are handled correctly. This includes the fifty or so tenants with kids I have scattered in town. Without my help, they won't make it."

"Susan, I just worry about you is all. And I will worry until you're gone from there, Paul is too unpredictable."

I was totally not listening, saying, "We have a lot to go over before I take the two-hour drive back to Edgerton."

I left important papers with her, other odds and ends along with some sentimental items.

As I got ready to leave she hugged me, "I'm so worried about you." Tears streamed down her face, "please stay safe."

I assured Kathryn everything was fine.

On the way home I took a detour to my childhood home. I hadn't been by the house in what seemed like years. The brick bungalow neighborhood, all in neat rows, looked the same. I smiled noticing that my handy work on the oak tree was still visible, the white coat of paint at the trunk in front of my old house. I recalled that my name was carved on the tree trunk, serving as a sort of permanent reminder to anyone that I was once there.

I wanted to get out of the car and walk around to the back of the house. But I chickened out, afraid someone would recognize me. I stayed a bit longer inside the car with my eyes fixed on the front door. I remembered every square inch of the house, going from room to room as if I were inside. Realizing there really weren't any good memories, I decided never to return.

The drive back to Wisconsin was peaceful. When I pulled into the garage at the house I was surprised to find Paul home.

"Surprise! Happy anniversary baby." There was that smile I hadn't seen for a very long time.

Paul had gone to great lengths to prepare the room with candles and freshly cut flowers. The table was set for dinner. Paul was freshly showered, shaved and wearing just the right amount of cologne.

I'd completely forgotten it was our sixth anniversary. It crossed my mind he could've sensed something about what I was doing, but I quickly realized his mood was also a result of some much needed cash he'd received on a deal to float operations another five weeks.

Paul hardly drank that night, his attention and focus was on us. I awoke the next morning to the aroma of freshly brewed coffee on the stove and Paul singing to me, something he hadn't done in what seemed like eons. He handed me a cup of coffee, still singing, "there are birds in the trees but I never heard them singing, no I never heard them singing 'til I met you. I love you baby."

"Everything okay?" he asked.

I replied that everything was fine, and how nice it was to see him in such a great mood. He thanked me for staying by his side through all of this, assuring me again, that, "We're almost there, just hang on my big broad shoulders."

I suddenly felt guilty, questioning whether I should continue with my plans to leave. Having a conversation with my favorite people—me, myself, and I—I tried to figure out what to do.

By Monday afternoon my thoughts quickly changed and I was back on track with my plans to leave. While in the apartment rental office Paul didn't ask, but demanded I wait for the banker who'd be arriving soon. I was to sign some additional paperwork which I realized would put us even further in the financial hole.

I refused to sign anything and we got into a heated exchange. I left the office and drove around for awhile before heading to the house.

While out driving I had gone down to the Rock River. The water flowed with such grace and beauty. I took off my shoes to stand on a slab of rock so the water could hit my feet. Standing there I looked up at the sky and found myself asking the same question, "God, why?"

I thought back to when my mother was still alive and then re-played the moment when I found her dead. I thought about lots of things, how things might have been different, contemplating what coulda, woulda, shoulda been. If only I'd gotten to the house sooner everything would be so different today, my mother would still be alive.

I shouted out to the river, expecting a response from God, but God had never answered me before so why should I expect anything now?

What I did feel was that I was doing the right thing leaving Paul. I mentally went through and crossed off all the reasons why I needed leave. A voice in my head assured me everything would be okay. I had no idea what I'd do once I returned to Chicago, but I knew that's where I needed to be.

Still standing in the river I realized it was later than I thought. Thankfully when I got to the house Paul was not there. A few hours passed before he stumbled from the garage into the house, roaring drunk, and slurring his words.

We continued to argue. I left, returning to the rental office at the complex where I worked most of the night.

The next morning Paul was screaming at me to wake up and finish our conversation. He made no bones about how disappointed he was in me for not doing as I was told.

I felt like a child being yelled at by her father. His words were like daggers to my heart. I didn't respond to his confrontational outbursts. I sat up in bed and stared at him prancing around the room trying to make his point.

When he asked what I had to say for myself, I shook my head, shrugging my shoulders. Finally I said, "Paul, I don't know what to tell you. Nothing I say, or do, will be enough. I suggest we table this discussion and move on."

His response was like a lion's roar. Spinning his head around in a full circle before he let spew a stream of raw anger, ending with, "You owe me an apology, which I expect by the time the day is over."

Paul stormed out of the house, banged the garage door shut, and headed to the construction site.

I stayed at the house for the day, deciding what I'd start to pack up what wouldn't be noticed by Paul.

In the garage there were some thick, heavy construction bags. I begin filling them up with clothes and hiding them in the down-stairs closet.

Later that evening when Paul returned I handed him his drink and I apologized. I'd decided this was the only way to maintain the peace until I left.

Paul didn't let up on me until he'd finally passed out for the night.

The following week I filled a vacant apartment with furniture and other items I had arranged to be picked up by Kathryn. There was so much to do besides maintaining my regular workload.

I knew I had one shot at leaving. Once I left there would be no possibility of returning or salvaging my marriage. I also believed if Paul learned of my plans the likelihood of me ever leaving while still breathing was highly unlikely.

Chapter Nineteen
Busted Compass

I was still on shaky ground, seconding guessing my decision to leave. I still loved Paul, but the price was too high to stay with him.

On the way to the office I stopped for coffee and headed to the Rock River, taking in its serenity. I realized, after helping thousands of other women successfully leave their spouses all across the country, I was now implementing the same plan of action for myself.

As the day to leave drew near it became clear why I was leaving. Paul's anger had spilled over to the tenants with explosive consequences. The city inspector and vendors refused to approve or conduct work on the site. Paul was out of control.

Kathryn came up for a visit the week before I was planning to leave. The three of us went to a crowded public restaurant, but while we waited for a table, Paul, who'd already had too much to drink, humiliated us. We ended up having to pick him up off the floor and guide him into the car.

Once I got him into bed, Kathryn was fuming over Paul's public display. Paul didn't remember much of the evening. While he lay in bed I packed some more of my things for Kathryn to take back with her. She was uncomfortable even staying at the house one night so she drove back to Chicago that evening.

During the night I continued checking off my long list of what needed to be completed before I left. It was difficult to sever ties with the victims of violence I'd been working with in Wisconsin.

I made sure the victims and their children in locations on and off the 13-acre site received extra gift cards for gas and food, enough to hold them over for a few months. I wanted to be sure to secure their needs in order for them to move on with their lives. Given my time restrictions, doing all of this was a tall order.

Both Kathryn and Daniel were upset at me for changing my date to leave until after Labor day weekend. Daniel screamed at me over the phone to stick with my plan, but my mind was made-up not to leave unitl after the court dates and safety issues for the women I was working with were in place.

The days and nights went by quickly and finally it was the day before I was to leave. I'd calculated for anything that could gone wrong. I stayed up most of the last night taking in the last memories of my Wisconsin home.

In the morning Paul hung around a little later than usual and I could barely keep my cool. Finally, an hour later than usual, he left. He kissed me goodbye and headed off to the construction site.

I gave myself one hour to pack up the truck. One by one I carried all the heavy bags from the cedar closet until they all fit flatly into the back of the SUV. With each trip back up the stairs, I stopped and thought about unpacking the truck, thinking to myself, I couldn't do this, that I didn't want to leave. Yet, I also heard a stronger voice telling me to keep going, not to stop.

Within an hour the SUV was packed. I checked the time and had one last cup of coffee. Again, thinking, maybe I shouldn't leave, maybe I should unpack, maybe everything would be okay.

Kathryn called my cell phone to ask if I was on the road. I hesitated, but Kathryn kept talking, "Susan, please remember why you're leaving … Susan are you still there … Can you hear me?"

In a quivering tone I spoke, "Kathryn, I'm scared. I don't want to go."

She encouraged me to keep going. Telling me I was almost there, just get into the car and she'd be waiting for me. I put my house keys, along with a prepared letter, on the counter for Paul.

I took the back roads out of town, making just one stop along the way at the police station. I left a letter with the Chief so he would know I had left on purpose. I was neither missing, nor had my car been stolen in case Paul decided to call the police.

Once on the Interstate, I began to cry. A few minutes later a State Trooper pulled me over, saying he could see something was wrong. He asked me if I was alright to drive. With my hazard blinkers on, the officer insisted I sit in his squad car for a few minutes until I was calm enough to continue driving.

When I was almost at Kathryn's, Paul called my cell phone. I let it go to voice mail. When I listened to the message he was crying, begging for me to return, "Please I'm very sorry for everything. You need a break honey, stay at Kathryn's for the weekend and come home on Monday. I can't do this without you honey, please hurry home."

I learned that a day or two after I left, Paul changed the locks to the house and office. In my mind any decision or change of heart I may have had was made easier knowing that he'd locked me out.

Leaving like this made it difficult to get my bearings in a new place. Most nights I didn't sleep, but tossed around thinking about Paul. Letters in care of Kathryn arrived from Paul every few days.

Over the next couple of weeks Paul continued to call, asking me to return. After about thre weeks I received a letter saying he had stopped drinking, "Now could I come home? He needed and loved me."

I missed Paul, but each day I told myself I needed to be strong and I couldn't go back. I still hadn't spoken with him. It wasn't time yet.

In an e-mail to Paul I requested he file the paperwork for the divorce. Paul replied by pleading with me, writing he needed help at the apartment complex so he could work on the financing with the banks. Was there anyway we could work something out? He added he wanted to talk to me.

Financing on the construction site would only happen, or so he said, if I'd come up and help with the tenants in the office for a few weeks. And if I didn't help we'd have to file for bankruptcy.

In the meantime, as I debated whether or not to see Paul, I re-connected with an old girlfriend and we made plans to meet for dinner in the city. At the restaurant she asked me what my plans were now that I was back in the city.

The next thing I knew she was scribbling a budget on the paper table cloth, offering me a job. Judy was the executive director of a large homeless agency. I'd be working at a new building, overseeing the case workers and clients. I asked about security access into the information system to locate my brother Bobby. She told me my clearance status would be able to show if he was alive and where to find him. I was more excited about trying to locate Bobby than the job. We agreed and I started work the following week.

I also contacted Daniel to discuss what had happened in Wisconsin. He was against me going back and then, after about an hour on the phone, changed his mind saying, "Actually, I don't know that you have a choice. Wisconsin is a marital property state and you'll need to find out just how much exposure you have."

I'd forgotten that my financial exposure was significant. The State of Wisconsin would give me half of everything by law in the divorce, but this was a house of cards waiting to fall. And the financial lenders on the businesses could still come after me for repayment of outstanding debts that on paper amounted to more than $20,000,000.

I had to sign over everything, knowing I'd still be liable because we were married. Daniel laughed, "want me to go with you? ... kidding! Susan see a lawyer first and weigh your options from there."

I didn't have any options. So, against Kathryn's objections, I drove back to Wisconsin.

This was the first communication between Paul and me in five weeks. I didn't know what to expect and I continued to tell myself everything would be alright, that I wouldn't let him smell my fear.

On the drive up I passed the apartment complex from the Interstate. You could see all the building cranes and dirt being moved. I knew that from here it was exactly twelve minutes to the house. I tried to stay focused, rehearsing what I'd say when I saw Paul.

I can't explain why, but while driving, for the first time in my life, I actually prayed to my own father, as if I were placing an order in the heavens. Maybe he could actually hear me? I'd forgiven him for what he'd done to my mother. I knew it sounded ridiculous to ask my father for help, but I was scared. I couldn't think beyond meeting Paul at the house. I realized I didn't really have a game plan. I was merely hoping for a sign that I could survive this dangerous dance with Paul. I wanted to believe my father and God, together, were going to watch my back while in Wisconsin.

As I got off the exit and rounded the bend, I drove down the single lane road to the house, along the back hole of the Edgerton golf course. I parked the car in the driveway and rang the doorbell. Paul grabbed me tightly in his arms and cried, then I started balling like a baby too.

An hour passed before we sat down in the living room to talk. He was going a bit overboard being kind and loving, it was uncharacteristic of him. Paul excused himself returning with several sheets of handwritten notes. He put his glasses on to read what he had written to me.

Paul's words focused on what an idiot he'd been and acknowledged that his expectations of me were unreasonable for one person to handle. Paul was sorry for not thinking clearly and for not seeing any of this coming. He was willing to do whatever it took to repair our relationship.

He went on to say how upset he was at me for leaving. He thought we should've been able to talk it out. Not communicating with him all those weeks was wrong of me, "You promised me you'd always watch my back no matter what."

Paul closed with how he knew his drinking was a problem. When he stopped drinking he realized how much clearer he'd seen everything.

Paul looked up from the pages and said, "I haven't had a drop to drink in three weeks. I'll never drink again, baby, on my father's grave I swear, please baby, come back."

I sat in silence and he stared back in silence, watching, and waiting for me to respond.

"Susan you can't just sit there, say something. Besides I can out stare you!"

My cell phone rang. "Don't answer it," asked Paul.

I answered it anyway. Kathryn was calling to check on me. I assured her everything was fine and not to worry. Paul scooted off the couch and slid over to me on his knees, placing his hands over mine and gently kissing them. Reaching up, touching my face, he said, "Susan, you're my compass, without you I'm lost."

I sat there knowing this was an unpredictable house of cards. A leopard doesn't change its spots to stripes. Like my father, with my mother, he claimed he'd do anything to get her back under his control.

Pulling from all my years of experience with victims of abuse and my own life I knew this was my most important test. It was me against a superior, master manipulator.

Again, as a flashback, I saw my own father. I understood that Paul shared many of the same characteristics. I realized that Paul's bright smile, which once drew me near was a mirror reflection of my own father. I remembered when I was married to Mark and how my parents behaved when we invited them to dinner, how my father had put on an act of kindness, just as Paul was doing now.

After talking it became obvious that it would be to my advantage to assist Paul with the business until the divorce was final.

In separate cars we went to the office and construction site. Paul said I could stay in one of the apartments. I informed him that I had a new job and started on Monday, but that I could come up on weekends to help. Every word and step I took was with extreme caution. My every move was like a bomb waiting to go off.

When I got ready to leave Paul grabbed me into his arms and again asked me to stay, "for us." He cried and pleaded, asking me to change my mind.

I caved in and stayed two nights at Paul's. In what was technically my own home I was now a guest. It was awkward. Everything I did that weekend, from getting up to get a glass of water and returning back to bed, to showering in the morning had a weird feel.

I went to the office and worked from there. Finally, I told Paul that it was time for me to drive back to Chicago. He made me swear on my mother's grave to return next weekend.

The drive home was bumper to bumper traffic. I got off the Interstate to take a more scenic route. Paul called to say how wonderful it was to see me and how much he loved me. When he referred to me as "honey" it grated on me, his words felt unnatural.

When I returned to the coach house there was a lot to do before I started my new job. I was up most of the night and on the phone with women in Wisconsin I was continuing to assist.

In the morning I left early and drove into the city for my new job. The next couple of days I was taken around to all the facilities to meet the staff and become more familiar with the inner workings of the homeless agency.

The building I was assigned to housed over 200 residents ranging from the homeless and various mental health situations, to independent living issues.

I was introduced to my staff, but to better gain their trust I didn't inform them that they would be reporting directly to me. I wanted to wait a couple of weeks. Unfortunately, I was not given the opportunity, on day three of the job there was a massive fire to the adjacent building.

I quickly implemented safety procedures gleaned from my time in Wisconsin. The fire was gaining strength and the tenants needed to be evacuated. I went floor by floor knocking on doors getting folks out, informing them to take their medicines and important documents with them.

We then started the task of placing tenants in temporary housing until well into the early morning hours. I ran home to shower and change. There was an emergency meeting with the agency's staff.

At the meeting Judy realized that the staff had no clue as to my position. After the meeting she asked why I hadn't told them? I explained the importance for them to get to know me first and gain my trust.

In moving the residents there were a lot of government regulations and lists of red tape to follow. Paul expected me to be back in Wisconsin on Friday. When I called and told him I couldn't leave until Sunday he was furious, screaming, "You promised to be here on Friday!"

I explained what had transpired at work and that I'd make this up to him. I left for Wisconsin in the middle of the night on Saturday and arrived Sunday at day break. Early Monday morning I drove straight back to work in Chicago.

When I got home to Chicago, I checked my e-mails. I spilled coffee all over my shirt in reaction to one of them. The e-mail read:

> Dear Susan: I don't know how to say this to you or if you will believe me, but I have wanted to contact you for a long time, but couldn't muster up the courage until now. My son is sick and I'm wanting to learn anything you're willing to share in regards to your family history. I know this is no way for anyone to learn something of this magnitude— I'm your half-sister. Your father and my mother were in a relationship many years ago. As a result of that union, I was born. There is much more I can share with you upon further contact if you're open to speaking with me. Thank you, Janet

I sat still, stunned in my chair, starring at the computer monitor. After thinking about it, I believed her and responded with a telephone number to contact me after 8:00 o'clock in the evening. The day flew by and I didn't give much thought to the news of a half-sister.

When the phone rang that evening we made small talk. I learned she'd grown-up in Rogers Park, not far from me and now lived in Texas with her husband and four children.

She was two years younger than me. Janet said her mother had no idea my father was already married when they'd gotten together and that the relationship had ended after the truth was learned.

We spent about an hour on the phone and decided we'd talk again the next night. We decided to look for family photos to send each other.

I contacted Kathryn to scan what few pictures I had and if she could make me a disk to send.

The photo Janet sent of herself was a dead ringer for my maternal grandmother. She was a blond version of myself. The photo of her mother and my father at an out-of-state wedding was eye opening. I could tell they were very much in love. Looking closer at the picture I realized her mother was the woman who arrived at the funeral home and laid a single white rose on my father's casket.

I didn't tell Janet that I'd briefly met her mother in person, it seemed pointless. We continued talking on the phone the next several weeks.

During one of my last trips to Wisconsin, Paul strongly urged me to go into counseling. His reasoning was that there had to be something wrong with me to just up and leave our wonderful life. He explained that my childhood had triggered things I had never dealt with. He was convinced I was suffering from post traumatic stress syndrome. He insisted that I dial the number of a mental health professional for a meeting that very day.

His tone of voice was that of a skilled psychopath. I played into his hand with the exception of contacting the therapist. I knew this game all too well. I'd seen my own father pull the same stunt on my mother, experienced this during my own custody case, as well as with those I provided assistance.

My goal was to be divorced and sever any and all communications with Paul as quickly as possible. Paul was at the desperate and dangerous psychopath stage. One wrong move or improper response on my end could potentially trigger the loss of my life.

The holidays were fast approaching and I continued to search for my brother. One of the case workers on my staff, Wanda, with whom I had formed a close friendship, devised a way to try and locate him. She called around to each of the agencies asking if Bobby had applied for any job skill classes.

Early one morning she barged into my office, "Susan, I found him. I know where your brother's living."

Wanda had a brilliant idea to send personal invites to all the other agencies and host a big Christmas dinner for agency residents all around the city.

Buses were arranged to host a Christmas dinner at our new facility. Wanda took care of all the details. As she left my office, she spun around and said, "I got your back, girlfriend."

I put in for Christmas work detail so that someone else would be able to spend the day with their family.

Judy called me into her office. "Susan, managers don't work on Christmas. Besides you're coming to my house for dinner. And I won't take no for answer."

I tried arguing with her, trying not to explain my reason for wanting to work that day, there was no convincing her.

On Christmas morning I went to work anyway. Wanda had called my staff and they were all coming in to help too. It was their present to me. I wouldn't know this until the dining room opened up to the general public, and each of my staff came in with the crowded buses. Each bus was filled with the homeless from various locations in the city.

Name tags were given out to the visitors prior to arrival. As luck would have it, Wanda was on the bus with my brother.

She ran into the building to find me. Out of breathe, she wanted me to brace myself, Bobby didn't look good and she was afraid of how I would take it.

I decided to stand at the side of the double doors leading into the dining room. The crowds of homeless men, women, and children were lined up in the lobby, waiting for their Christmas dinner. Wanda jumped up from behind the crowd and pointed to Bobby. As he inched his way along the dinner line I moved closer, wondering if he would recognize me.

My heart sank. Bobby looked the same as those men I had served for Thanksgiving dinner so many years before. His hair was matted. Most of his teeth were missing.

I did everything I could to keep from crying. I had to be very careful. If Bobby didn't recognize me on his own, I didn't want to jump at him and say, "It's me, Susie, your sister." I was sure the sudden and unexpected event would prove too traumatic.

As Bobby passed me, there was nothing. I ran in back, behind the counter where the food was being served, put on an apron and gloves, and bumped a person out of the way so I could serve Bobby food when he arrived.

I said Merry Christmas to everyone I handed a plate too. When I handed Bobby his food, and said, "Merry Christmas," he didn't look up, he just replied, "Yeah man, happy Christmas, thanks for the food."

Devastated and trying not to cry I moved my eyes elsewhere to compose myself. When I looked over to the far corner of the dining area my entire staff was there and to my surprise Judy had shown up.

Judy came up behind where we were serving food, and asked me to come with her.

"Susan, we'll figure out how to help him, for sure, now that we know where your brother is living. Come on let's go, you have to help me cook back at the house."

As we walked out, Judy said, "this has to be one of the best Christmas presents I've ever witnessed."

Chapter Twenty
Flying Without a Net

Janet contacted me after the holidays, she wanted to meet with me in Chicago. After much thought, I declined. For the first time I realized the pure horror of our lives. There was too much pain already, meeting Janet would only add salt to a wound I had no interest in revisiting, a place buried deep inside me I realized was hell.

Paul called me and said he had something important we needed to meet and talk about. He tried to persuade me that we could not go through with the divorce.

Paul explained that he'd secured top notch lawyers because of a criminal investigation regarding the properties and projects on the entire business and they had advised him not to go through with the divorce as well.

I asked him to read to me, over the phone, or to send me via fax, what he had in the way of paperwork. Paul, in true manipulator fashion, stated, "No, we need to talk in person."

Paul speculated about who could've turned him in and surmised it had to be a former sub-contractor. I didn't understand what he was talking about.

I asked him to explain more and he turned his conversation into some prolonged, crazy song and dance. Then asked me to call the law firm now representing us.

"Am I named in those papers?" I asked.

Paul didn't answer me.

I didn't know what to believe.

Paul then threatened me, saying, "If you don't drive up to meet with me immediately, I'll put the brakes on the divorce."

"I need to call a lawyer first, give me a few days." I decided not to contact anyone in Wisconsin until I knew what was going on.

Immediately I began reaching out to folks in the legal community for input. I hoped whatever was happening wouldn't affect me.

The following morning things were hectic at the agency. The security desk paged me over the intercom to come up to the front lobby, "There are some visitors here to see you."

I couldn't imagine who it could be, so I called the front desk to find out. Security told me two government agents were in the lobby from Wisconsin.

I took the elevator downstairs to see what they wanted. I instructed them to follow me into a private room. Apparently an official investigation had been opened with regard to financial matters in Wisconsin.

When the agents finally left I went upstairs to Judy and showed her what I'd been given. She read through the documents and told me not to worry, "Everything will be okay, this has more to do with Paul than you."

I contacted Daniel, informing him that I'd just been visited by federal agents from Wisconsin. Daniel reassured me that my name was on the paperwork only because we were married.

I still didn't understand. If I was no longer in Wisconsin why they would drive all the way to Chicago?

Daniel said Paul had finally pissed off someone and now the Government had opened an official investigation.

What Daniel never mustered up the courage to tell me was that he was the person who'd meet with the US Attorney's office along with his wife who happened to be a forensics accountant and assisted with the investigation.

I was livid because I had truly trusted Daniel and valued his input and guidance. Daniel talked me into enlisting the assistance of his accountant wife to perform certain accounting functions a year prior to leaving Paul. This had just been a disguise to gain access into the financial accounting of the combined businesses. I'd never known Daniel's plan was to use me to get back at Paul over a soured deal between the two of them. In doing this Daniel ensured I'd be joined like a Siamese twin with respect to whatever was going to happen to Paul and the allegations against his businesses. The government's investigation was based solely on Daniel's wife sneaking around like a spy, taking confidential documents in an attempt to discover illegal activity with the lenders, partners, banks, and government.

I contacted lawyers I knew and set up meetings. Then I contacted Paul, he laughed when I told him that two government agents had paid me a personal visit.

"Not to worry honey, they're just on a witch hunt. And that's why we need to talk about all this to see what we're going to do to make it go bye-bye," he said to me.

Paul insisted I speak with his lawyers, but I declined for the time being until I knew more about what was happening.

After meeting with a lawyer in Chicago, I was referred to a former federal agent who looked over everything. He asked me for some additional financial documents and we arranged another meeting. In his professional opinion, they were going after Paul and the company accountant, not me.

Examing our tax returns we also learned that I'd never owned any of the properties or businesses. I was shocked at this. Upset that I'd been played by Paul from the very beginning.

By the time I talked to Paul next, he had no clue that I'd figured things out. He called, telling me that I needed to come back so we could, in his words, "fight this together."

My response to Paul was that I'd done nothing wrong. He started threatening me and tried to turn the conversation around as if I was the reason nothing was working out.

I refused to play his game.

Paul then informed me, "at the direction of my lawyer I will not give you the divorce."

In my mind this wasn't going to be a problem. The paperwork for the divorce had been filed a few months before any of this financial garbage had begun.

I had to drive to Wisconsin for our first hearing on the divorce. Paul had added language to the divorce documents basically throwing me under the bus. He claimed that I'd take responsibility for any outcome from the government's case.

In private, outside the courtroom, Paul again asked me to return home and drop all this nonsense.

"You're sick honey, let me help you, I love you. We need to be able to fight this together, it's the only way all of this will be resolved, trust me baby," he pleaded.

I responded by telling him, "I wanted nothing, I owned nothing, and to just let me walk away and move on."

He refused.

My lawyer filed another motion for a continuance on the grounds that we were unable to reach an agreement.

On the drive back to Chicago Paul called several times, but I didn't answer. I also decided, even after discovering what Daniel had done, to speak with Daniel, remembering it never hurt to keep your enemies close. Although Daniel was no longer my friend, I wanted to keep the lines of communication open because he'd known Paul for a number of years and could still help me.

Daniel suggested an overall action strategy which included a much needed pep talk. Anyone who knew me knew I was a wimp when it came to any type of confrontation. Which was funny because I'd never had a problem standing up for victims of violence, but when expected to do so for myself I backed down.

With Daniel's pep talk fresh in my mind, I called Paul right away, the first words out of my mouth were, "Listen and don't speak!" Then I continued, "You're divorcing me otherwise I'll go to the financial partners and enlighten them on what's going on with their precious investment. Ten bucks says they haven't a clue. And I'm willing to bet another twenty that you've used the fact that I've left you as your bullshit excuse to buy more time in milking the banks and partners for more money until your precious financing is finalized."

Paul attempted to speak, but I continued, "I'm not finished! At the next court date if you do anything to stop the divorce, it won't be pretty. And further interference from you will cause me to react in a way you'd never expect!"

I slammed the phone down so hard its cradle broke in half. Paul stopped his threats and calls.

I decided that after this fiasco with Paul was over to give my notice at the agency. I wanted to go back to working with victims of abuse and stalking, full time.

After receiving an unexpected e-mail from my son, we arranged to meet for breakfast at my girlfriend's restaurant downtown. I hardly recognized him. He'd grown so tall. Our meeting was awkward. We hadn't seen or spoken to one other for nearly a year. He wanted to know if I'd give him money for his prom. I hesitated for a moment before deciding to tell him I'd moved back to Chicago. I had hoped we could build a relationship now that he was older. When we said our goodbye's he promised we'd meet again in a few weeks.

In the meantime, I focused on getting my brother Bobby into a more suitable living environment. I'd now seen that because of our horrific childhood his life was forever altered in a way no one could have predicted.

It's no accident that my work with the homeless population taught me to understand that when trauma occurs the time clock in their lives stop.

Over the weekend Kathryn and I made plans to get together and have dinner. I was mentally exhausted from everything that had happened. We talked about God. I asked her how she continued to be a faithful servant, because I couldn't be.

Kathryn explained to me that, for her, God gives us no more and no less then we can handle.

"Well, I must be the exception," I said, "because I'm done. Really, Kathryn, I can't take this anymore. All I want to do is go home and be with my mom."

Kathryn snapped back at me. "Stop talking like that, you're not going anywhere. God's been with you each step of the way. You don't get to pick and choose the shinny shoes you wear on your journey in this lifetime."

There was a long pause before I responded, "is it really so wrong of me to want to go home? To take the elevator up to heaven and be with my mom? I miss her so much."

Kathryn believed, saying, "good or bad, everything was in accord with God's timing."

"Frankly, I've never been one to subscribe to that way of thinking," I replied.

"Susan, you need to stay here until you've accomplished God's purpose for your life and when God is ready, you're name will be called."

I didn't understand, giving her a give-me-a-break look. I still questioned, as I did during Sunday school when I was child, if we're good, why does God allow bad things to happen?

Vincent's father contacted me shortly after I'd met my son for breakfast. When I politely inquired as to where Vincent would be attending college, he didn't respond. Instead hr tried to extort money from me. When I wouldn't play ball, he warned me, "I'd be sorry."

My son and I met again for breakfast, but all he cared about was how much money I'd give him towards a new car. Sadly, it was clear Vincent had no interest in me other than as a source of money.

When I didn't give him what he wanted, he responded with angry verbal attacks. I was devastated. Somehow, with Paul's assistance, Jeff had been able to forge my name on court documents, to unseal and make public the divorce records.

As if that wasn't enough, Jeff filed additional bogus documents resulting in monetary judgments. I refused to play into the hands of both Paul and now Jeff. I didn't react. Instead, I focused on returning back to Wisconsin and finalizing my divorce. The following month I drove back up to Wisconsin not knowing what to expect. Our respective lawyers had continued to do battle over the language in the divorce decree.

Briefly, I met with my lawyer instructing him that I wanted this all over. I had no intention of returning to this courtroom. By the afternoon I took the stand and was sworn in by the judge. The only issue left to verify, for the record, was that I wanted nothing from the marriage.

Finally, the judge tapped his gavel on the bench and granted the divorce. The gavel also represented another death to me. An ending to a life I'd created with a man I'd loved with all my heart. It had been a safe place over a period of years in which I'd called home, but now it was all erased.

I quickly left the courthouse parking lot and drove to my favorite spot on the Rock River. The whoosh of the water gently jumped up onto the rocks and back down again. I took off my high heels, allowing the water to caress and sooth my aching feet.

I said a prayer in hopes that God was listening, "that though all of this hell would He take me by the hand and finally let me come home?"

Standing, listening to the water, on top of my favorite rock, I heard my cell phone going off in the car.

I took a deep breath and walked over to answer another call from a victim for help. My eyes looked up to the bright blue sky, I realized at that moment that God was holding my hand through hell.

Epilogue

"Yea, though I walk through the valley of the shadow of death, I will fear no evil: For thou art with me"

There is a survivor's guilt within me. It takes a hold of me most nights as I try, in vain to sleep. Ever since the deaths of my parents I have consciously worked to jump-start joy, but how does anyone jump-start something that was never really there in the first place? I'm here to tell you that knowing when to get out of my own way is no walk in the park. I find some days so dark no amount of light shines through. There are days I'm unable to see.

I never imagined so many would perish and be hurt in such painful ways in this world—never. I never imagined so much suffering in courts. I never imagined so much sorrow just to love another, never imagined there would be such heartache just to love my own son, to love a husband. Not only have I have walked through the shadow of death, but I feel like I've pitched a tent and set up camp in this valley.

I go forward knowing that God is holding my hand through hell. I live with the thought that God must have a plan for me. I find room to smile from time to time with the solace that I'm here to help others receive the justice they deserve.

Acknowledgements:

Jane Palombo, you took me out from the storm and gave me shelter. You are truly an angel.

Kathryn McBride, who guided, directed and supported me through the years, unconditionally.

Dirk Wales, for never giving up on me, even when I'd wanted to give up on myself. I'm a lucky dog!

Diane Fanning, your never ending love and support of me and my work has allowed me to go farther than I could have ever dreamed.

The Honorable Nancy Sidote Salyers, a true friend, who has always supported my journey.

Pastor Neil Schori, God certainly broke the mold when he sent you to me. I am humbled and honored by your dedication and friendship.

Barbara Hardin, we've had one heck of a journey together and I'm eternally appreciative of everything you've done. You are my hero!

Ward Foley, my long distance guardian angel who watched over me when I didn't have the strength always from your lips to God's ears.

Jillian Mass-Backman, your unwavering support and love is truly a blessing.

Sandra Brown, MA, for your friendship and lighting the way on the highway to solutions that is changing the world.

Holly Hughes, my amazing legal eagle and colleague who pushed and encouraged me through many a storm.

Amy Matthews, who always answering the phone at all hours of the night and listening as I went through endless changes and edit's.

Rick Davis, an amazing mentor for teaching me how to get out of my own way.

To my colleagues and supporters for justice, Robin Sax, Michael Houbrick, Chester Hosmer, Karen Elkins, Claudine Dombrowski, Isabelle Zehnder, Gayle Crabtree, Peter Hyatt, Donna Gore, Denny Griffin, Dr. Laurie Roth, Jay Cleveland, Wanda Jefferson, Dr. Deborah Breed, Carole O'Neil, Sheryl McCollum, Michelle Harkey, Kelly Osborn, Holly Lofland, Kelly Walker, Betty Houbion, Robert Rahn, Felix Nater, Burl Barer, Howard Lapides, Dr. Scott Bonn, Quintin Wilcox, Christy Davis, Connie Braddock, Bridget C Lewis, and Kim Anklin thank you each for all you do in your lives unselfishly for others.

Monica Caison, you're tough on the outside, but on the inside, your heart plays a symphonic melody of truth and love. Thank you for all you do!

To my Legal Beotch, without you, none of this would've been possible. In spite of your smart ass ways, you still managed to do the impossible!

To my son Vincent and kid sister, I'm here just as I've always been, waiting to put the past to rest and embrace the future!

Susan Murphy Milano is a specialist and expert in intimate partner violence and works nationally with corporations, faith based organizations, domestic violence programs, law enforcement, and prosecutors providing technical and consulting services in "high risk" domestic violence and stalking related cases. Her principal objective is to intervene before a victim is seriously injured or killed. Utilizing a procedure which she devised, *The Evidentiary Abuse Affidavit*, Murphy Milano's clients are all still alive—a statistic that is remarkable considering the distinct increase in intimate partner homicides.

In addition, she and her work have been prominently featured in newspapers, magazines, radio, and television including: *The Oprah Winfrey Show, Larry King Radio, ABC'S 20/20, Justice Files, E-True Hollywood, CNN, Sunday Today Show Profile, Women's Day, Family Circle, US News and World Report* to name a few. She has frequently participated in guest media commentary panels on major news programs and recently appeared on the A&E Biography of Drew Peterson. She is a well known radio host, regularly hosting *The Susan Murphy Milano Show, "Time's Up!"* on the Zeus Media Network, also she appears on *Crime Wire* on BlogTalk Radio, and is a regular weekly co-host on the nationally syndicated *The Roth Show*.

Her books, *Defending Our Lives; Moving Out, Moving On; Times Up!* and corresponding strategies are taught world-wide and used by law enforcement, social workers, attorneys, health care workers, human resource departments, and domestic violence agencies.

The Ice Cube Press began publishing in 1993 to focus on how to live with the natural world and to better understand how people can best live together in the communities they share and inhabit. Using the literary arts to explore the wide variety of lifestyles and experiences in the heartland of the United States we have been recognized by a number of well-known writers including: Gary Snyder, Gene Logsdon, Wes Jackson, Patricia Hampl, Greg Brown, Jim Harrison, Annie Dillard, Ken Burns, Kathleen Norris, Janisse Ray, Alison Deming, Richard Rhodes, Michael Pollan, and Barry Lopez. We've published a number of well-known authors including: Mary Swander, Jim Heynen, Mary Pipher, Bill Holm, Connie Mutel, John T. Price, Carol Bly, Marvin Bell, Debra Marquart, Ted Kooser, Stephanie Mills, Anna Lappé, Bill McKibben, and Paul Gruchow. We have won several publishing awards over the last nineteen years. Check out our books at our web site, join our facebook group, visit booksellers, museum shops, or any place you can find good books and discover why we continue striving to "hear the other side."

Ice Cube Press, LLC (est. 1993)
205 N. Front Street
North Liberty, Iowa 52317-9302
steve@icecubepress.com
www.icecubepress.com
@icecubepress on twitter

Holding the hands of
two loving miracles
Fenna Marie & Laura Lee